The Reminiscences of
Roger L. Bond

Interviewed by
Paul Stillwell

U.S. Naval Institute • Annapolis, Maryland

Copyright © 1995

Preface

Several years ago, Commander Thomas Buell, noted naval historian and author, suggested that I interview a friend of his named Roger Bond. Commander Buell was living in Minnesota at the time and had come to know Mr. Bond through attending the same church. Bond's stories of his service as an enlisted man during World War II were so captivating that Buell felt they should be preserved through the medium of oral history. Fortuitously, the Oral History Association held its annual meeting in St. Paul, Minnesota, in October 1987, and I was able to take advantage of the opportunity to do the interviews. The result is a valuable contribution to the source material available on the enlisted experience in the war.

Mr. Bond was a teenager when the United States entered World War II in 1941. The following year he turned 17 and soon enlisted in the Navy. Even before that he had already begun training for such an experience by participating in the sea scouts in southern California. Soon after his enlistment, he went through recruit training at San Diego, California, and then reported to the destroyer Saufley. Illness caused that tour of duty to be a short one.

After his recovery, Mr. Bond joined the crew of the aircraft carrier Saratoga and served on board from 1943 to 1945. His descriptions of life in "Sara" comprise the heart of this engaging memoir. Detailed wartime recollections from enlisted men, particularly individuals as articulate as Mr. Bond, are rare in the literature. He provides vivid word pictures of living conditions on board an old ship, camaraderie among shipmates, participation in battles, the professionalism of the quartermaster gang, leadership from officers, liberty experiences, and vignettes from service with British naval forces in the Indian Ocean.

After his departure from the aircraft carrier, Mr. Bond served in the patrol craft PCE(R)-858 in 1945-46. Afterward, like so many others of his generation, he earned his college degree under the GI Bill and then went on to a successful career in the civilian world. In this telling of his history, Mr. Bond serves as a representative of the hundreds of thousands of young men of his time who went off to serve their country at sea at a time when it was waging a successful fight against overseas aggressors. Commander Buell performed a useful service is recommending that this story be preserved for the benefit of history.

In the course of moving from the initial raw transcript of the oral interviews to this final version, both Mr. Bond and I have done considerable editing in the interests of accuracy, smoothness, and clarity. I have added footnotes to provide additional information for those using the volume. Ms. Ann Hassinger of the Naval Institute's history division has made a significant contribution through her diligence in the overall process of printing, proofreading, and overseeing the binding of the completed volumes.

                                                Paul Stillwell
                                                Director, History Division
                                                U.S. Naval Institute
                                                September 1995

Authorization

The U.S. Naval Institute is hereby authorized to make available to individuals, libraries, and other repositories of its choosing the transcripts of two oral history interviews concerning the life and career of the undersigned. The interviews were recorded on 16 October 1987 and 17 October 1987 in collaboration with Paul Stillwell for the U.S. Naval Institute.

The undersigned does hereby release and assign to the U.S. Naval Institute all right, title, restrictions, and interest in the interviews. The copyright in both the oral and transcribed versions shall be the sole property of the U.S. Naval Institute. The tape recordings of the interviews are and will remain the property of the U.S. Naval Institute.

Signed and sealed this _____ day of November 1995.

Roger L. Bond

Interview Number 1 with Mr. Roger Bond

Place: Hotel St. Paul, St. Paul, Minnesota

Date: Friday, 16 October 1987

Interviewer: Paul Stillwell

Q: To begin at the beginning, Mr. Bond, could you please tell when you were born and provide a description of your parents.

Mr. Bond: I was born in Milwaukee, Wisconsin, June 19, 1925. My mother was born and raised in Milwaukee. My father had moved to Milwaukee from East Tennessee. His family had been in Tennessee since it was part of North Carolina, and he'd come north and settled in Milwaukee.

Q: What sort of business was your father in?

Mr. Bond: My father was in the hosiery business and at that time, mostly in sales. He'd always been in the textile business and my grandfather too.

My mother's father had been in the Navy in the Civil War. I think she always had a sort of a soft spot for the Navy, because we always seemed to visit naval installations and naval ships when we traveled. And we did travel a lot,

Roger Bond #1 - 2

because both my parents liked to travel. I remember visiting the dirigible <u>Akron</u> in Florida in 1932 and the <u>Macon</u> in California in '33.* We moved to Los Angeles in 1933, when I was eight. I recall one time that year when we were visiting San Francisco. The fleet was in, and we visited the aircraft carrier <u>Saratoga</u>. My mother took a lot of pictures, which were sort of significant later on when I served on the ship.

Q: What was the occasion for the visit?

Mr. Bond: I can't remember what the holiday was. It probably was the Fourth of July.** I think it was that summer because I wasn't in school. The fleet was in San Francisco and anchored in the bay, and visitors were visiting all the various ships.

Q: It's interesting that you should happen to visit that particular ship.

---

*Both of these rigid airships were soon lost. The <u>Akron</u> (ZRS-4) crashed at sea in a storm off Barnegat Light, New Jersey, on 4 April 1933. The <u>Macon</u> (ZRS-5) crashed into the Pacific off Point Sur, California, on 12 February 1935.
**During that era, the U.S. Navy's Battle Force was based at San Pedro/Long Beach. Ships often visited other West Coast ports on holidays so people could go aboard for tours.

Mr. Bond: Yes, and my mother was almost an archivist the way she kept pictures. In 1943, when I went aboard the <u>Saratoga</u>, she sent me those pictures of the ship.

Q: What details do you remember from that visit, being eight years old at the time?

Mr. Bond: Well, not a whole lot. I remember being fascinated by the fighter planes at that time, which were F4Bs, very small biplanes.

There was a Marine that was very friendly and showed us around the ship. I do remember going down to the ship's service and the big ice cream fountain counter, which had a marble top. In the tiled front it had a picture of a rooster, which was the crest of the <u>Saratoga</u>. It was still there when I went aboard ten years later. In 1933, as I recall, they served a larger variety of items in the ship's service than during the war, when it was pretty much just ice cream.

Q: Was the ship fancier then than during the austere wartime?

Mr. Bond: Oh, yes. For example, there was linoleum on the decks, and it was just immaculate.

We visited a lot of ships in the Long Beach Harbor,

too, over a period of years. None of them made that much impression on me, but a large part of the fleet was based there.

Q: Did you visit any of the battleships that you recall?

Mr. Bond: Well, I know I was on the Colorado. I really didn't gravitate so much to battleships. We were on a number of destroyers and cruisers when I was a kid, but I just can't recall what those ships were.

I was certainly bent towards the sea in that period, so when I was about 15 I joined the Sea Scouts. Los Angeles was very fortunate because of a gift received about that time from a man named Peterson who was retired from being vice president of Standard Oil. He donated his yacht to the Sea Scouts for a training ship. It was a 64-foot gaff-rigged yawl named the Corsair, which had been built in Stavanger, Norway. He pensioned off his captain who so loved the boat that he donated his services to the Sea Scouts and was commissioned as "Commodore of Training." The captain's name was Herman Larson. He was a German of Swedish extraction and had served all his life in deep-water sailing ships. And I seemed to get along very well with Larson, perhaps because I could understand broken German-English better than the average southern California kid. I was used to hearing it in Milwaukee.

Roger Bond #1 - 5

Q: What had been the impetus for the move from Milwaukee to southern California?

Mr. Bond: Well, it was an opportunity my dad had to become a western states distributor for the hosiery mill he worked for. He had to move to someplace in the West, and Los Angeles was a large market. Ironically, my mother did not want to go to San Francisco because she was afraid of earthquakes. I don't think San Francisco's really had an earthquake since then, but Los Angeles has had a number of them.*

Q: So you understood this fellow's broken English.

Mr. Bond: Yes, and the more excited he got, the more the English became disguised with German pronunciation. He was a great influence on me. He was a perfectionist of a sailor, and he was meticulous all his life. Anybody can splice rope, but he taught me how to splice wire too.

Q: Why is it more difficult to splice wire?

---

*The devastating San Francisco earthquake of October 1989 was two years after this interview was conducted. The most recent in the Los Angeles area was January 1994.

Mr. Bond: Well, for one thing, you have a lot more strands, and you do it with the lay instead of against the lay. And, of course, you need a large fid to open up the wire.* Also, most cables have a rope core. As the wires stretch, they squeeze against this hemp core instead of weakening the strands. Then it's an organizational job. The wire's got a lot of tension built into it, so you have to keep it secured all the time that you're working it and not just let it generally fly apart.

We did a lot of other things too. Larson was convinced that the best thing to grease a U-shaped shackle pin was mutton tallow. So every year we rendered a number-ten can full of mutton tallow for use during the year. From the old sailing ships days he was used to doing everything aboard. I think he'd have made a new suit of sails if it was required.

Q: So he taught you seamanship essentially.

Mr. Bond: Yes, he taught me seamanship essentially and a lot of little things: how to scull a boat and just all kinds of small work and fancy work with rope yarn. He was quite an influence.

---

*A fid is a sharply pointed round wooden tool used to separate the strands of line or wire rope so they can be joined with others in a splice.

Captain Larson used to decry the fact that I was too old to go to sea, because from his perspective, once you became older than eight or nine years of age, you'd been ashore too long to adapt to a seafaring life. And I'd say, "Well, I'm not really that old, only 16."

"Oh, no, you've slept in a bed too long now."

Q: What did he teach you about the commonality among sailing ships?

Mr. Bond: When the merchant service had sailing ships, the crews were international. When someone was paid off on one ship, he went down to the shipping office and signed on another ship. Whether you got off a Greek ship and went on a Norwegian ship, or went to a French ship--it was immaterial. Most sailors knew all the parts of a ship in at least six or seven languages. They might not know anything else except seamanship. Because of the way the crews were hired, it was absolutely necessary that all ships be rigged the same, and these crews made it that way. They ensured that every ship was rigged identically in every way that mattered. By that I mean there might be some little detail that had nothing to do with the working of the sails. You had peculiarities, but, as an example, the foretopsail buntline was secured to the same pin on every ship.

Those seamen traveled all over the world, but they really weren't travelers. The ships were their homes, and their homes traveled. They just lived on the ships and knew very little about what else was going on. Larson was quite an exception to that because history was his hobby. In most of his career he was an officer, and he was the captain of several ships.

One ship that he was the captain of was the <u>Renée Rickmers</u>, which was a four-masted bark. He told me that he was in northern Chile to load nitrates in 1914. There'd been unseasonal rain, although I guess any rain is unseasonal there. Anyway, there were no nitrates to load, so the owner sent the ship to New Caledonia to load nickel ore. While it was at sea, World War I broke out. At that time what is now American Samoa was German Samoa. A German naval squadron was present. It was not very large, but it was large enough in comparison with the other forces in that area so that it was a worry.

The French blacked out the lighthouse that was at the entrance to the barrier reef to New Caledonia. This was the New Caledonia Amité Light--Friendship Light. The ship made a surprise landfall just about a mile and a half from the light and piled up on the reef. That was significant later on, because I finally had a chance to go to New Caledonia during World War II. We were entering that passage by the lighthouse, and down about a mile and a half there was a rusty hulk with a bowsprit pointing up. The junior officer of the deck said, "I wonder what ship that is." I was able to tell him it was the Renée Rickmers and that I knew the captain that put it there, so it certainly is a small world.

Q: What became of Captain Larson after he piled that ship up?

Mr. Bond: Well, he was, of course, interned. The French gave him his parole, because he was a civilian, and he was allowed to go. He arrived in the United States, near San Francisco, in 1915. He decided he didn't really want anything to do with the German military adventures, so he applied for U.S. citizenship. With his skills, he became chief rigger of a shipyard in San Francisco. It was at that place that this man Peterson became acquainted with him in some way and hired him. He went to Norway and supervised the building of the yacht Corsair. Of course, that's one reason that he was so attached to the boat, because I would guess that he selected personally every piece of wood that went into it. That was his way. It was a beautiful bit of craftsmanship.

This yacht had a mainsail with a very heavy gaff, and about six of us young fellows would hoist that sail with its gaff. We would get it as tight as we could, and he could then stretch it out the last couple of inches by himself. Of course, he knew how to pull, and he was a very vigorous man.

Larson was 80 years old in 1940 when I first met him. He did not have a tooth missing in his head. I don't think he had any fillings. He bought a new 1940 baby blue club coupe and drove it like he was a high school kid.

He died when I was away in the Navy. That was in 1944, which would make him 84. I understand he just went to sleep one night and didn't wake up, never really had a sick day. He was really a wonderful old guy, a role model and example.

Q: Sounds as if he had a great influence on you.

Mr. Bond: Oh, yes, he did, especially in that area of seamanship. He was like a father in the sense that if you came from a maritime family, then your father showed you these things and brought you along. My dad was not a seaman and wasn't much interested in that. In that area, Herman Larson was my father, and then I left him to join the Navy.

Q: Before we get to that, I'd like to talk some more about your boyhood. How much of an impact did the Depression have on your family?

Mr. Bond: My dad was able to earn a fairly good living during the Depression. We did not really experience a lot of want. I didn't realize at the time how fortunate I was. We would not spend a lot of money or do a lot of extravagant things, but we had what we needed.

Q: Would you call yourself middle class in that context?

Mr. Bond: Yes, I'd say middle class.

Q: And your dad worked steadily?

Mr. Bond: Yes. Basically his pay was commission, but he did have a good following and was able to earn a good living.

Q: People still have to wear clothes in a Depression.

Mr. Bond: That's right. One thing that's interesting was that he was a very early advocate of flying. Of course, the western states that he covered were long distances. He wanted to cover all the major customers, and so I remember going out to the airport to meet him. This started even before we moved to California, because I remember meeting him aboard Ford Tri-Motors and Curtiss biplanes. I remember how thrilled he was the first time he was in a DC-3 because you could walk up the aisle standing up.* The aisles were really getting big.

Q: Did your mother encourage your continuing interest in the Navy as you grew up?

Mr. Bond: Oh, yes, although it wasn't so much the interest in the Navy as interest in seamanship. When other kids were talking of going to different colleges, I decided I wanted to go to the California Nautical School at Vallejo.** I wanted to become a merchant marine officer. That was the influence of Larson. He was not very pro-Navy because the only naval experience he had was in the German Imperial Navy. When he was conscripted in the Navy, he was already a mate, but because of his birth station and all, he could not be an officer. However, they did recognize his ability and put him on the sail training ship as a boatswain or boatswain's mate. He didn't like the Navy very much, so maybe subtly he slanted things more to the merchant marine.

Q: But that was enough to steer you away from, let's say,

---

*The Douglas DC-3 went into service in the mid-1930s as perhaps the first really successful commercial airliner. Designated C-47 by the Army and R4D by the Navy, the plane was a much-used transport during and after World War II.
**This institution is now the California Maritime Academy.

the Naval Academy.

Mr. Bond: Well, that was part of it. I have sort of strange eyes. If you test either one of my eyes separately, they don't test very well, but they seem to compensate. I had to really squint to see 20/20, so I had the feeling that I could not go to the Naval Academy.

Q: But wasn't it even an ambition when you were a boy?

Mr. Bond: Not so much, although my mother would have liked me to go to the academy. That's why we visited Annapolis when I was a boy. She was a very patriotic American. She was the kind that thought you ought to visit Washington, D.C., and since you were there, it was only a short way to Annapolis. And we were ecumenical; we visited West Point, too, once. But Mother always rooted for Navy in Army-Navy games, that sort of thing. But I guess I just didn't quite set my sights on the Naval Academy.

My mother had a very close friend who was married to a man that was in the academy class of 1916. He resigned from the Navy, but he was still very interested in naval things. When I went into the service, he gave me his academy ring after he had the stone flattened and had a fouled anchor mounted on that stone. I had that ring with me all the time I was in the Navy. I didn't wear it too

Roger Bond #1 - 14

much, because it was a very heavy ring and I was a little bit self-conscious. It did create a comment or two at times, especially from older officers who recognized its age.

Q: Why would he give it up?

Mr. Bond: Well, I think, he felt that if I was going to war and took his ring, that gave him a connection with it.

Q: You were taking his place.

Mr. Bond: I was taking his place.

Q: What was his name?

Mr. Bond: His name was John Rough.* He was a Cornishman, originally from Michigan.

Q: How good a student were you in those growing-up years?

Mr. Bond: Well, I was a pretty good student, in that I always took a heavy academic program. I took physics, chemistry, solid geometry, trigonometry, and all that. But

---
*In pronunciation, Rough rhymed with Howe. He entered the Naval Academy with the class of 1916 but left the service prior to graduation.

Roger Bond #1 - 15

I didn't get really outstanding grades because I was sort of occupied with other things. A lot of it was activities like Sea Scouts and that.

One thing I really enjoyed was drafting. I went to Los Angeles High School, and we had an excellent drafting teacher. It was a lot of fun. I kept taking drafting because I enjoyed it so much, which has come in handy in several places--being able to read blueprints and all. It's interesting, however, when I was interviewed to go into the navigation department of the Saratoga, the one thing the navigator asked me was whether I knew anything about optics. I said, "Only from physics classes and all." That satisfied him, and he accepted me. I never figured out why knowing anything about optics had any bearing on my duties, but it was something he seemed to use as a qualification question for some reason.

Q: Well, you might have to do something with binoculars presumably.

Mr. Bond: Oh, sure, we used long glasses, and the sextants had glasses in them. But one thing I did learn to appreciate was my drafting training.

But, anyway, getting back to time in school there, I also worked on a yacht in the summertime, an 87-foot schooner. When the war started, the Navy began taking in a lot of private yachts, and that schooner was slated to go into the service. I remember we took sort of a farewell trip over to Catalina Island in January 1942. In southern California in January you can get some nice days and nice weekends. We went over on just a super Saturday with a good, spanking breeze and really put the ship through its paces, and it was a ship too. Then Sunday was a very calm day, and we came back and we sort of drifted home. It was a nice farewell.

While coming back we noticed planes dropping dummy depth charges on a submarine in the channel there. On that beautiful, quiet day it brought home to us why this was a farewell trip.

The man that owned that ship had a fellow working for him that really was very experienced in sailing ships, had been brought up in Maine. The condition that the ship would go in the service was that he would go along as the skipper. He was a Naval Reserve officer, but the ship went in the Coast Guard, and he was transferred to become a Coast Guard officer. He wanted me to join the Coast Guard and tell him when I went to boot camp. After boot camp he wanted me to be assigned to this ship, the Seadrift. I didn't think that was really such a good idea, because it was no way to fight the Japanese.

Q: Did you have any other jobs in your growing-up years?

Roger Bond #1 - 17

Mr. Bond: One thing about the Depression was that men had most of the jobs that kids have today. But I did have paper routes. In fact, the morning I went into the Navy, I delivered my last paper. Twice a week I was delivering the shopping news, which was a good job for a high school kid. I wasn't tied down every day.

Q: What are some examples of jobs that kids have now that men had then?

Mr. Bond: Well, men worked in the equivalent of fast-food restaurants, as parking lot attendants, and stockboys in the food markets. But I will say that from the paper route, I think I had more usable income than most of these high school jobs nowadays, allowing for inflation and that sort of thing. I delivered the L.A. Times, and I lived in a Republican sort of neighborhood, so there were only about six houses that didn't take the Times. I'd make about $35.00 to $40.00 a month. In the late '30s that was a pretty good amount, because $10.00 a day was top wages; that was foreman's wages for men.

Q: Were you involved in any sports in school?

Mr. Bond: Yes, mostly I ran track and cross-country. I

went out for football, but in our school we had a complicated setup. Los Angeles schools had varsity, B, and C sports. Your age got so many points, your height got so many points, and your weight got so many points. The idea was that if you were a B or C, you wouldn't be competing against the big kids. But at our school, we had about 30% Japanese kids. When they were 18 years old, they still were so small they were playing B or C. In fact, our C football team was all Japanese except for one Jewish kid who was the center. And they were not immature kids. They were 17 or 18 years old, two-year and three-year lettermen. My first day out for football we didn't scrimmage. The second day I thought it was an accident; the third day I knew it wasn't and changed to cross-country.

Incidentally, in the fall of 1941, L.A. High won the league championship in football. They beat Venice High School, 13 to 12. A second-string halfback by the name of Yoneji Fukinaga--and don't ask me to spell it--passed for one touchdown, ran for another, and kicked the extra point. So in a 13 to 12 game, that was pretty vital. Less than two months later he was in a relocation camp, Camp Mansinar.*

---

*Shortly after the Japanese attack on Pearl Harbor in December 1941, individuals of Japanese extraction--including those born in the United States--were relocated from the West Coast to inland internment camps. The U.S. Government feared they would sabotage the American war effort. In the 1980s the government paid compensation to the Japanese-Americans because of the relocation.

Now, this reminds me of that Japanese relocation. I know very well that we were absolutely stunned and shocked by it, and this went for the teachers, the student body, everybody else. They talk nowadays about people being caught up in anti-Japanese hysteria and all, but those of us that were around were not. We were all very upset and disappointed that our classmates were gone. We were sure that people would come to their senses so these students could be back next semester. Of course, it didn't work out that way.

Q: What was your relationship with your Japanese classmates in the late '30s?

Mr. Bond: Oh, I'd say the relationship was excellent. There were quite a few of them on the track team too. In our district we had one Boy Scout troop that was all Japanese kids. The first time I ever saw sukiyaki was when we were at a camp-o-ree held in Griffith Park in Los Angeles. We spent a lot of time preparing our meal and a lot of time cleaning up, and these kids had some strange dish that they just whipped up in a very short time. They ate it with chopsticks, licked the chopsticks, and cleaned out one plate. They were out playing again, and we were still scrubbing pots and pans. I thought to myself they knew something that we didn't know.

Q: How much were you paying attention to world events as the dictatorships grew up and the Japanese advanced in China?

Mr. Bond: Well, I paid a lot of attention, because, as I said, I delivered papers. I think I started delivering papers about the time Germany marched into the Rhineland.* And I followed the war; I'd always liked maps. My dad was an avid, avid reader. In traveling, he almost always brought home a book or two that he'd bought on the road, and the house just accumulated them. He was interested in history; he was interested in current events and world affairs. We always discussed that sort of thing in our house. So I followed it, and I remembered the maps published in the papers when Hitler moved into the Sudetenland and into Memel and all those events.**

Q: I would say that you inherited that love of reading and love of history from him.

---

*In 1936 German troops occupied the Rhineland, which had been demilitarized following World War I to provide France a buffer against attack.
**In 1938 German Chancellor Adolf Hitler annexed the Czechoslovakian Sudetenland as part of Germany, and in 1939 he took Memel, an East Prussian port that had been awarded to Lithuania following World War I.

Mr. Bond: Oh, there's no question about it. And then, of course, when I got acquainted with Larson in the Sea Scouts he just didn't stop at seamanship. When the sun went down or you were eating, he didn't want to waste that time, so he would quiz us on history. Of course, he had been all through Europe, and he told us about the events leading up to World War I. He felt the situation in World War II was a continuation of the situation in World War I. I learned a tremendous amount of European history from him.

I remember very well one article that I read, probably in '39 or '40. A fellow was off China, near where the Yangtze River meets the ocean, and he observed a Japanese aircraft carrier operating there, recovering and launching aircraft. This fellow was a former U.S. Navy pilot who had operated off of aircraft carriers. I remember that article saying that the Japanese were the second-best carrier pilots in the world. It said they were just downright on a par with the Americans in the speed of recovering those planes and launching them, and he said the Japanese were far, far ahead of the British, who were the only other ones operating aircraft carriers. That was sort of a warning, because we didn't associate quality with Japan in those days.

Q: Where did you read that article? That's intriguing.

Roger Bond #1 - 22

Mr. Bond: I think I read it in an aviation magazine. One thing kids used to do in those days was spend a lot of time in a drugstore reading magazines and nursing a Coke. Or a group of us would get one Pepsi Cola with three glasses of ice. So a lot of my current event reading was there. But that did make an impression on me because it was so contrary to the accepted practice. You'd see pictures of Japanese soldiers usually, and they were sort of funny-looking guys with wrap-around puttees and baggy pants. They didn't seem like they were very serious. But operating those aircraft, to me, was very illuminating. That wasn't funny at all.

Q: What was the reaction in your community when the Panay was attacked in late 1937?*

Mr. Bond: I can remember that very well. I know in our family there was a lot of shock, and as I recall, my mother felt we should teach those Japanese a lesson right then and there. My dad was a little more cautious on it, saying that there were more ramifications to it than that. But that made people aware of those gunboats like the Panay. And I'll tell you, The Sand Pebbles was really one of my

---

*On 12 December 1937 the Yangtze River gunboat USS Panay (PR-5) was attacked and sunk by Japanese aircraft near Nanking, China. Two crew members were killed and 43 wounded. Japan claimed it had made an error in identification and paid an indemnity for the incident.

favorite Navy movies.* That was the old Navy, and it was the best portrayal I've seen of the China station in any movie.

Q: It is a marvelous picture.

Mr. Bond: Right down to the dress whites.

Q: When you're speaking of the dress whites, that was the enlisted uniform that had the jumper with a blue collar flap.

Mr. Bond: Yes, the blue collar and the blue cuffs. And, of course, one of the things that was really a treasure when I was in the Navy was somebody who still had a set of dress whites. He couldn't wear it anymore, of course, but it gave him an awful lot of seniority.

One day when I was 17 I was talking with Jim Mitchell, someone I'd run track with and one of my best friends. He was also in the Sea Scouts with me. He was a little bit older; he was soon going to turn 18, and he wanted to join

---

*The Sand Pebbles was a popular 1966 motion picture starring Steve McQueen, Candice Bergen, Richard Attenborough, and Richard Crenna. It was based on Richard McKenna's novel of the same name, published in 1962 by Harper & Row. McKenna served in the U.S. Asiatic Fleet shortly before World War II, including two years on board the gunboat Luzon (PR-7).

the Navy. So on a Monday he suggested I enlist too. I said, "Well, I don't want to join the Navy."

He said, "Well, why not? You were going to do it, anyway."

I said, "Well, I might join the Coast Guard."

He said, "No, the Navy is a much better place. It's got more opportunity. My cousin's in the Navy, and he said it really is important to go in the Navy with a buddy, so that you have a friend at boot camp. And then, you know, we'd probably stay together for a long time."

Q: Did your parents try to influence you in any direction?

Mr. Bond: No, not really. My dad was away at that time. But after that remark on Monday, the following Saturday I was sworn in. I'm not really sure how everything happened so quick, but I know my dad's approval came by telegram. So there really wasn't a lot of difficulty getting my parents' permission.

Q: Well, I would think especially not your mother's.

Mr. Bond: No, that was easy. I think she probably persuaded my dad if he needed any persuasion. My dad was in the Army in World War I in France, and he always looked upon it as a very muddy experience. He thought the Navy, at least, was a lot less muddy than the Army. So maybe he thought that would be a good deal.

Q: What was your experience with the recruiting station?

Mr. Bond: We went to the recruiting station at Beverly Hills; you might as well go in style. This was a small recruiting station, and the fellow in charge was a chief. He said, "Well, do you guys want to join the real Navy, or you want to join the reserve Navy?"

"What's the reserve Navy?"

He said, "Well, you know, if the country's being invaded, they call up the reserves."

"No, we want to join the real Navy." So he enlisted us as USN. We didn't realize until we got down to boot camp--and found that people had different kinds of serial numbers--that the reserve Navy had already been called up. The chief forgot to tell us that that happened several years before.

Q: It would also make a difference in the time period of the enlistment, wouldn't it?

Mr. Bond: Yes. The other guys had ID cards that were valid for the duration of the war, but ours had specific dates on them. Since I was 17, the expiration date was the day before my 21st birthday.* But it worked out about right, anyway. I figured it was just about the same as if I'd been in reserve. It was a good thing for me when I was involved with older men who were regular Navy. Most people I was with in the Navy thought I would never leave. They thought I was a 30-year man for sure. I guess I just kept my options open. I didn't make that decision until it came close to time to leave, and I left because of an opportunity to go back and go to college.

Q: Had you finished high school when you enlisted?

Mr. Bond: Yes. I had finished high school.

Q: Well, that's sooner than most. Most people finish at 18 rather than 17.

Mr. Bond: Yes, that's right. I was a little ahead on that basis.

One time when I was home on leave, later in the war, I went down to USC.** I was in the admission office, and what I was really interested in was whether I could take correspondence courses from the Armed Forces Institute and

---
*Bond joined the Navy on a minority enlistment, which expired 18 June 1946. Because he was not yet 18 years old at the time of enlistment, he had to get his parents' consent to join.
**USC--University of Southern California, a private school with its campus in Los Angeles.

have them count as college credit. If I'd been going to the university, then I would have a record started, and the correspondence courses could be applied on it. They said, "Why don't you just make out an application?"

I said, "Well, how could I? I don't know when I can come."

They said, "Well, just make out the application and for date of enrollment say, 'Will advise later.'" And so I did. When I decided to leave the Navy, it was when all the veterans were coming home, and the universities had huge waiting lists. I sent a letter to USC and said, "I submitted my application in December 1943. I'd like it to apply for the fall semester of '46." I got a registration permit in the return mail. It just clicked, so that was a good piece of advice.

Q: Sure. Had your option regarding a merchant marine career evaporated when the war started?

Mr. Bond: Yes, I think so. I thought of the merchant marine as a peacetime occupation, and I wasn't particularly desirous of fighting the war from a merchant ship. I don't mean to degrade the contribution made by the merchant marine, but I felt that if it was going to be wartime, I wanted to serve in the armed forces. In fact, I wasn't even interested in being in a Navy gun crew for a merchant ship. I wanted the fleet service.

Q: Did you have to go through any testing process at the recruiting station?

Mr. Bond: No, not at the recruiting station, other than a preliminary physical. I don't remember any impediment whatsoever. Maybe it was because I was a high school graduate, but there was no problem. When we got to boot camp, we went into detention, which was a kind of quarantine. Of course, we took all sorts of classification tests and things of that type, but we were already in the service then.

Q: What was the reason for the quarantine?

Mr. Bond: Well, the first three weeks you were in an isolated camp, Camp Farragut in San Diego. I suppose if you had any infectious diseases or anything like that, then they kept you from infecting the entire station. Actually, it wasn't really so effective a quarantine because we shared the ship's service with recruits who were already outside. We came in one door, and they came in the other, but you were milling around in the same room. But it did isolate us.

Roger Bond #1 - 29

I think some of it had to be part of the psychological thing, so you had a little bit of space to yourself. You weren't off with the general recruits, the old salts that had been there a month. That's really the way you thought about it. My gosh, somebody had been there a month; a man was really an old-timer in two months. You could just tell by the way they walked.

Q: Did you have any difficulty adapting to the regimentation of the Navy life?

Mr. Bond: No, not a bit. When I was in high school I was in the ROTC all the way through.* In the ROTC you wore a uniform four days a week, and you paid a $2.00 deposit for the uniform. If it was complete at the end of the year you got back a buck and a half, so for 50 cents I could be clothed for four days of the week. I was a terrible ROTC cadet. I was the first three-year private they ever had.

Q: Why was that?

Mr. Bond: I just wasn't interested in the Army.

I got to be an embarrassment in the third year because there was no program for a third-year private. So then I got to work at the rifle range with a sergeant that was

---
*ROTC--reserve officer training corps.

there. If I'd known that, I would have deliberately aimed to be a three-year private because we had a lot of fun. We fired on an indoor small-bore range. Despite my overall attitude, I did understand close-order drill, the 1903 Springfield rifle, and those sorts of things. So when I went to boot camp, that part of it didn't faze me at all.

Q: It probably gave you a leg up on the straight civilians.

Mr. Bond: Yes, it did, it really did. So that would have eliminated a lot of emotional shock, although we didn't do a lot of drilling. Our company commander was a chief gunner's mate, and he felt that he was preparing each one of us to be in a 5-inch gun crew. So when other companies would drill, we'd work out on loading machines.

Q: Well, his approach made a lot more sense.

Mr. Bond: I think so. I think so.

Q: What sort of a guy was he? Was he a harsh taskmaster?

Mr. Bond: No, he was pretty cut and dried, and he wasn't going to be your buddy. I don't remember any resentment whatsoever.

Now, in those days, organization of the seabag was very strict, just the way we rolled our clothes and tied them with clothes stops. The clothes were stenciled just in the right place and all that. You laid it all out for seabag inspection. We scrubbed our own uniforms, and if yours were dirty, why, you had to lay out the contents of your seabag, and the chief would march the company across your uniforms. You got involved with that sort of thing.

Q: That didn't happen more than once to an individual, I would guess.

Mr. Bond: No, no, I don't recall it ever happening twice to the same guy.

Q: It was a lot of incentive to get clean.

Mr. Bond: Right. He used certain kinds of techniques like that, but there was no malice whatsoever. And he definitely felt that he had to prepare us for duty in the fleet. It never entered his mind that any of us would end up as a mechanic taking care of a Coke machine in a shore station. He was a real Navy man and thought things should be done the Navy way. He wasn't erasing any of the Navy traditions just because there was a war on. He thought that was the natural way; whether in war or peace, it

Roger Bond #1 - 32

didn't make any difference.

Q: Well, that would probably be all the more reason to teach these Navy traditions.

Mr. Bond: Right. Also we were inculcated with the idea that there were right-arm rates and left-arm rates.* It was much preferable to have the right-arm rates.

Q: Gunner's mate was certainly one of those.

Mr. Bond: Gunner's mate was one of them. As I recall, it was boatswain's mate, turret captain, gunner's mate, quartermaster, signalman, fire controlman, and torpedoman's mate.

Q: Was it his influence that got you into a right-arm rating?

Mr. Bond: No, I already wanted to be a quartermaster. That was the highest rate in the Sea Scouts. They ran theirs a little bit differently, but a quartermaster in the Sea Scouts is the same thing as an Eagle Scout in the Boy Scouts.

---
*Rating badges for a few of the traditional Navy ratings were worn before and during World War II on the right sleeves of enlisted men's jumpers and blouses. All the rest were worn on left sleeves. Since World War II all enlisted rating badges have been worn on left sleeves.

Q: I see.

Mr. Bond: I never made quartermaster because you had to have senior Red Cross lifesaving, and at that time I think you had to be 18 to have that. So I had everything but that. I had to settle for the real thing instead of a Sea Scout.

Q: Had you passed the swimming part of the scout test?

Mr. Bond: Yes, I could do that. I had my junior Red Cross lifesaving. When I was in boot camp, we could see the signal school and quartermaster school, and I could pretty well read anything I saw in semaphore there.* At that time I didn't read the light too well, but I could read the semaphore just as fast as they were sending it when I went into the Navy.

Q: What were the living conditions like in your barracks?

Mr. Bond: Clean and simple. A lot of the fellows that I talked to had gone to boot camp just before the war. The

---

*The Navy employs three basic types of visual signaling: semaphore, using a pair of flags at each end so that various arm positions represent different letters; Morse code, via flashing light; and flag hoist, in which a different colored flag stands for each letter or number.

barracks just had stanchions, and they had swung a hammock between the stanchions. But we had bunks. The basic barracks in San Diego had been there for quite a while, and they were stucco, Spanish-style buildings. They were very nice buildings, I'd say. There was no privacy. I mean, those were the days when the whole company slept in one big, long room with all those rows of bunks.

Q: How much attention was there to military appearance and keeping your uniform in good order?

Mr. Bond: Well, in boot camp there was a lot of attention to that. The military bearing, clean and neat--probably more so than anyplace else that I saw in the Navy.

Q: Did you have daily personnel inspections?

Mr. Bond: At the very least, I would say. The company commander inspected several times every day. We went everywhere in formation. We had at least a cursory inspection. This fellow Jim Mitchell that I joined the Navy with was from a Scotch family, and he had the thickest, strongest beard that I've ever seen on a young fellow. We had a regular Saturday inspection, and we'd be inspected about 10:00 o'clock. His beard grew so fast that he already had a 4:00 o'clock shadow and always got demerits. When we cleaned up the washroom, we had to leave a path so that at the last minute, Jimmy could go in and shave and then we cleaned up the path when we got out. So that, I guess, illustrates the fact that we had a lot of attention to that.

Navy boot camp wasn't as extreme as the Marines went through, but there was quite a bit on getting everybody down to basic entities and building group morale. They tried to eliminate all differences that you might have brought in from civilian life. Actually, in our company there were only about six or seven guys from California. Most of the rest were from Oklahoma and west Texas. They weren't very sophisticated, but that didn't make any difference. We were all the same there.

Q: Were most of them less well educated than you?

Mr. Bond: Yes, I'd say most of them were quite a bit less educated. Probably only about half that company had graduated from high school. For a number of them the biggest body of water they'd ever seen was a stock tank.

One thing that shocked me quite a bit was swimming. We had to swim a distance, and it was very minimal. There was nothing to it, but that was a terribly hard thing for about half that company. The incentive that they had in those days was that the chief just said, "Well, you won't

Roger Bond #1 - 36

go on liberty until you do this." We had guys that went all the way through boot camp and never got liberty because they never passed the test. I'm sure it was only something like 25 yards. It was a very easy swim for anybody that had any knowledge. If you could dog paddle, you could dog paddle the distance.

That just really shocked me. I'd never come across that, because I can never remember not knowing how to swim. Of course, living in Los Angeles and being there from eight on, I really spent a lot of time on the beach. The year before I went in the Navy I only missed one day that summer at the beach, which was the advantage of having a morning paper route instead of an afternoon paper route.

Q: Well, of course, that's so vital to possibly saving a guy's life if his ship were sunk.

Mr. Bond: But even today I run across people, especially here in Minnesota, that do not know how to swim. Usually it's somebody that's middle-aged or more because with all the pools in the school system now, the kids are learning to swim. But that really did astound me, such an easy swimming requirement they couldn't pass.

One thing that worked out sort of well for me was the small-bore rifle competition. All those mornings I spent in the ROTC rifle range really came in handy, and I did win several extra liberties for small bore. We used a standard government small-bore rifle that weighed the 8.67 pounds with a balance. A lot of these guys never were familiar with that rifle. It was just like I had owned one for a couple of years, so I did well.

Q: Did you have a position of leadership in the company?

Mr. Bond: Well, I was the platoon leader for a little while, and I guess my immaturity sort of came out one day. We were going to go and draw the rifles, and as I went down the storage rack, I turned all the cutoffs up on the rifles. We were soon afterward in a formation with rifles, and the first thing was inspection arms. I would say about 100 out of 156 bolts hit the dirt. I was the only one laughing, so I was demoted to the assistant mail orderly. It was an impulse act.

Q: It must have taken you a while to carry out that impulse.

Mr. Bond: Oh, no. I used to check all the rifles. I just went along and turned those cutoffs up on the end of the bolts, and not one guy noticed it.

Q: What was the curriculum at boot camp?

Mr. Bond: Well, the curriculum centered around a lot on physical fitness, a lot on basic seamanship familiarity. Of course, a lot of it was just drumming into you the fact that you were in a different environment and using nautical terminology: ladders, bulkheads, overheads, decks, and so forth. We did a lot of rowing of whaleboats, which was mostly for physical fitness, but also it gave us a sense of being on the water in a boat.

Q: And it builds that unity that you were speaking of.

Mr. Bond: That unity, that's right. As I said, our company spent a lot of time on loading machines. We attended a lot of lectures.

Q: What did they cover?

Mr. Bond: Well, they covered what I'd call the old A to N in The Bluejackets' Manual, just general things.* We had some seamanship classes in basic knots or things like that, and basic semaphore, although I can't imagine why we covered that. I think that was more calisthenics and the

---

*The Bluejackets' Manual, which has been published by the U.S. Naval Institute in various editions over the years, has long been considered the "bible" for Navy enlisted men. It is a basic textbook and reference volume on a wide variety of naval subjects. Formerly these topics were addressed in chapters designated by letters from A to N.

other 156 guys going "A, front; B, front; C, front."

Q: Did you have ship recognition, for example?

Mr. Bond: No, not really.

Q: Lookout training?

Mr. Bond: No lookout training. I would say it was pretty much military drill. I know one time here recently we were discussing sex education. Tom Buell was in this conversation, and we were talking about when we were growing up just nothing was said of it.[*] I mentioned the fact that the only sex education class I was ever in was taught by a chief gunner's mate. It was, "Stay away from those kind of girls."

Q: What kind of girls did he mean?

Mr. Bond: The kind of girls that you caught diseases from.

Q: Were there training movies as part of the curriculum?

---

[*]Commander Thomas B. Buell, USN (Ret.), is the author of biographies of Fleet Admiral Ernest J. King and Admiral Raymond A. Spruance. He is a friend of Bond and recommended him as an oral history subject.

Mr. Bond: No, just lectures.

Q: What about health and hygiene for those who, perhaps, weren't as sophisticated?

Mr. Bond: Well, there were classes in health and hygiene, and the sex education came in one of those series of classes. There was just a whole lot of attention on cleanliness, and that's really why all this emphasis was made on spotless clothes and all; it was to build the cleanliness habit. You can get away with certain carelessness in a civilian situation where you're not very closely packed. But in a Navy situation and close living and the density of people, it just is intolerable. You just can't put up with dirtiness, and, of course, infestation of lice or something like that would be terrible on a ship.

Q: Presumably you'd be more susceptible to infection if you were wounded and not clean.

Mr. Bond: Oh, yes, that too. That's right.

Q: Did the topic of homosexuality ever come up?

Mr. Bond: Never, never. Not in that era.

Anyway, we took these classification tests and took an eye test, and the eye test eliminated me from going to quartermaster school. I had scored very high on mechanical aptitude because the whole mechanical aptitude test was built on a Model A Ford. I had a Model A Ford and used to take it apart and put it back together again. The Navy test had things like a picture of the carburetor or some other Model A part and said, "What is this?"

So I was slated to go to motor machinist's mate school. In the meantime, they moved us to Camp Decatur, which was part of that naval training station. It was sort of a holding place for waiting until school was opening up. We were doing seaman guard duties and things like that, just being useful, and waiting for school. Then, all of a sudden, one day they came in and said, "Pack up. You're moving out."

Now, the fellows in our company that had lower classification scores were just assigned to sea duty and sent home for sea leave. But before they got back, we were moved out and moved down to a labor pool at the San Diego destroyer base. They were pulling these four-stackers out of the red-lead fleet in the back bay.* We were chipping the red lead off of them, and also off some old S-class submarines. I wanted nothing to do with submarines after

---

*Red lead is the nickname for an orange-colored anti-corrosive primer paint applied to bare metal before the regular paint is put on.

working on the ones at San Diego, even though they were old and nothing like the fleet submarines used in the war.

Q: Had you graduated from boot camp?

Mr. Bond: I'd say we were sort of ejected more than graduated. I mean, at this time there was such a pressure of in-bound people that you just got shoved out the other end to make room. That's why we were sent down to the destroyer base.

That base was an interesting place in those days because it was commanded by Captain McCandless.* He swarmed all over the place, usually in dungarees. One story goes that McCandless looked inside this packing crate one day, and there was a sailor sort of curled up reading. McCandless had a dungaree shirt on. He just peered around and said, "Gee, you found a good hiding place."

The guy said, "Yeah, it's really a good place. I've been using it for over a week."

McCandless said, "You have? What do they think you're doing?"

"Oh, they think I'm working down there on that S-boat, but there's so many guys, they can't keep track of it." And then the man said, "What are you doing?"

---
*The commanding officer was Captain Byron McCandless, USN (Ret.) who was recalled to active duty for the war. The frigate USS McCandless (FF-1084) is named in honor of the captain and his son, Rear Admiral Bruce McCandless.

McCandless put on his cap, and he said, "I command this station."

From then on, I assure you, that sailor was not lost in the crowd; he contributed.

The great thing about this destroyer base was the food. Generally speaking, one of the guys going through the chow line was this old guy McCandless in his dungarees, and he'd better get a good meal. The mess cooks serving the food didn't seem to recognize him, because they changed all the time. The cooks probably knew him, but the food was served by the mess cooks.

Q: How did the food compare with what you'd had at boot camp?

Mr. Bond: Well, I won't complain about the food at boot camp, but the food at the destroyer base was a lot more varied. We were doing a lot of work, and they would feed working people. It was sort of a nice transition place to get used to the feeling of being in the Navy without being shoved into a particular billet yet. But then we got ejected from there and sent over to Pearl Harbor.

Q: Before we get there, maybe we could talk about liberty in San Diego. You knew how to swim, so presumably you had that opportunity.

Mr. Bond: Yes, that's right.

Q: I know that many merchants there really preyed on young sailors on liberty. Did you encounter them?

Mr. Bond: Yes, but you have to remember that we were awful young. The first thing they did when we got in the Navy was tell us to send all our civilian gear home because the Navy would give us everything we needed. And they gave it to us, but they also deducted for quite a bit of it--not that you had your choice. When you're making $21.00 a month then they deducted from that, our first payday was $6.50. And so then we'd spend some.

I do remember the first liberty. We went into town, and there were three of us. One was my best buddy, Jimmy Mitchell, who was of Scottish derivation. We figured Jimmy would have some money, because he was so conservative he wouldn't be spending his money at ship's service like we were. Each of us bought two bus tokens for a quarter so we had our return fare, and we caught a bus to downtown San Diego. We went to a show, and then after the show we said, "Why don't we pool our money and have something to eat?" We didn't have any money and neither did Jimmy, because he sent his home.

We did have enough money to buy a loaf of bread, a jar of peanut butter, and a quart of milk. So we sat on the steps of a grammar school, and we spread the peanut butter on the bread with our ID cards. After that we walked around town, and we finally decided that there just wasn't anything you could do in San Diego without any money. So we used our tokens, went back to the base, went over to ship's service and bowled, or something like that.

After that, when we got a liberty, we'd go up to Los Angeles, because we always had 36-hour liberties on weekends.

Q: So you could go home then.

Mr. Bond: Yes, we could go home. I have a sort of liking to surprise people, so one time I didn't tell anybody I was coming. No one was at home when I got there, so I went over to my best friend's house. Nobody was there, so I went over to my girlfriend's house. Nobody was there, so I went over to another fellow's house; he wasn't there. I went to another guy's house; he wasn't there.

Back of him lived a girl named Marilyn Williams that I had gone with for a while in the early years of high school. She'd recently had a very serious operation, and I knew she was recuperating. She was still in high school because she had lost a year from this operation. I dropped by to see her and had a nice visit. It was the first time I'd even talked to her for a year. Her dad had died, too, the first part of the year. It just so happened she wanted to write to a sailor, so she wrote to me. That's the gal I married after the war, and I'm still married to her. So if it hadn't been for my wanting to surprise people, I probably wouldn't have dropped in on her and reacquainted myself and all that stuff. A little twist of fate.

Q: You were just desperate to surprise anybody.

Mr. Bond: Yes, I was running around looking for somebody to surprise.

Q: Did you have any typical sailor-type liberties in San Diego?

Mr. Bond: No, I was way too young. You could not get into any bar in San Diego unless you were 21. California was very strict in that, and there just wasn't any use trying. You could not falsify a Navy ID card at that time, not the one they issued there at the destroyer base, which was a laminated card.

We didn't do anything like that. We went to the beach a couple of times, but actually we had more fun on the base

Roger Bond #1 - 47

because they had good recreational facilities.

Q: Would you explain, please, that term ship's service you used? What did that encompass?

Mr. Bond: Well, ship's service was really the service to the crew of the ship or station. Aboard ship it might be nothing much more than a little store where you could buy candy or something like that, and on bigger ships ice cream. But at shore bases they'd have bowling alleys, pool tables and things of that sort. The Craven Center at the Bremerton Navy Yard was really pretty sophisticated and better than anything in town.*

Q: Well, and probably deliberately so to keep people away from the less scrupulous merchants.

Mr. Bond: That's right. But, you know, there's also a lot of psychology of wanting to get away from the place. But once you've done that and you've walked all over downtown and had your peanut butter and all, there really wasn't very much to do. I never did get out to the zoo at that time, although it was a good zoo even in those days. I don't know why, probably because nobody else wanted to go,

---
*Bond was at the Puget Sound Navy Yard, Bremerton, Washington, later in the war when his ship, the carrier Saratoga (CV-3) went there for repairs and overhaul.

and I didn't go alone. I would say that San Diego was a very overwhelmed town in the summer of 1942. The service personnel, Navy and Marines, really were very numerous. It was a much smaller city in those days too.*

Q: I just saw in the paper today that it passed a million for the first time.

Mr. Bond: Of course, they've annexed everything within reach. But that was quite an emotional shock when they passed San Francisco, and that was several years ago--the last census, I believe, '80. But I don't recall anything with liberties in San Diego except that one time when we had that peanut butter and bread and milk.

Q: How did you get from there out to Pearl Harbor?

Mr. Bond: Well, we went out on a destroyer tender that was going that way. We arrived at Pearl and reported to the destroyer base there at Pearl City. We got a terrible shock when we got there. It's sort of hard to believe, but when the attack on Pearl Harbor was made, about the only news that was released was the Arizona was sunk and the Oklahoma was badly damaged, and other ships were damaged in several degrees. And, of course, they'd admit that the old

---
*The census of 1940 reported San Diego's population as 202,028.

Utah, which was a target ship, was sunk. But there weren't any details, and none of the pictures were out. Even being there in San Diego, you did not hear about it.

Q: It didn't really come out until the first anniversary.

Mr. Bond: And the words, of course, didn't have the impact of pictures. That's probably the thing that did more than anything else to change people's minds about Vietnam—because there they were moving pictures. When we went into that harbor, there was still a lot of damage and a lot of oil. They were vacuuming on that harbor clear into '44, I think, because they had practically no tide, and it's a very narrow entrance. So that just shook us when we found out how much damage had been done.

After I was there a while, then I was assigned to the USS Saufley, which was DD-465.*

Q: Had your duty at the destroyer base in San Diego gotten you type cast as a destroyer man?

Mr. Bond: Yes, I think that was sort of it. Although I had known other people that had gone through there and were

---

*USS Saufley (DD-465) was commissioned 29 August 1942. She had a standard displacement of 2,050 tons, was 376 feet long, and 40 feet in the beam. Her top speed was 37 knots. She was armed with five 5-inch guns, ten 40-millimeter and seven 20-millimeter guns, and ten 21-inch torpedo tubes.

assigned to different duties, I think that was sort of a pipeline at that time.

The <u>Saufley</u> was almost a new ship, less than a year old. She was in the <u>Fletcher</u> class, which I've always thought of as sort of the flowering of the destroyer.*

Q: Many people share your opinion.

Mr. Bond: It had a lot of the old classical attributes of a torpedoboat destroyer brought to its finest conclusion. They were going machines, and the <u>Saufley</u> was a particularly fast one. When she'd get up there at 38-39 knots you could stand on that fantail, and it was just like being on a speedboat.

Q: Kicked up quite a rooster tail, I would imagine.

Mr. Bond: That's right. On the fantail all you could see was water around you, stern waves and all. You really had a feeling that you were in a high-class operation, and I just really enjoyed it. I was in the first division, and on a 5-inch gun crew, just where my boot camp company commander wanted me to be.

---

*The class took its name from the USS <u>Fletcher</u> (DD-445), which was commissioned 30 June 1942. Comprised of 175 ships, it was the largest class of destroyers in U.S. Navy history. The design was developed on the eve of World War II and thus was used for wartime mass production.

Q: I don't think we really covered what a loading machine did back there at boot camp. Could you explain that, please?

Mr. Bond: A loading machine simulated the breech of a 5-inch/38 gun except that when the rammer pushed the round home, the ammunition just passed through and fell out the other side.* In the 5-inch/38, you had a projectile and a powder case. You'd put them into a tray, and then the rammer rammed them in. It was just a super gun, and those guys really spent time with their guns. The performance was so impressive that after having experience with one of our antiaircraft cruisers, the San Diego, the Japanese reported one time that the Americans had devised a clip-fed 5-inch gun.**

Q: The practice you got on that loading machine made you better at creating that impression of rapid fire.

Mr. Bond: Oh, that's right, and it got me assigned to that job. I'd rather been there than some of the other duties down below.

---

*The 5-inch/38 had an advantage over previous 5-inch guns in the U.S. Navy in that it was dual-purpose, able to fire at both aircraft and surface targets. The Fletcher-class ships were armed with five single-gun mounts; later World War II-built destroyers had three two-gun mounts each.
**The 5-inch/38 single mount could fire approximately 15 rounds per minute per barrel.

Q: It's really a matter of teamwork.

Mr. Bond: Yes, that's it; it's a matter of teamwork because, you know, everything has to arrive together and flow to have that fire volume. So, anyway, I enjoyed being on the Saufley, but one thing I realized was that I was really buried in the first division. Even as small as a destroyer is, my horizons were very limited there. Of course, I was very junior, and you just didn't get involved with other divisions and other spaces on the ship.

Q: Were you a seaman second class then?

Mr. Bond: Yes, I was a seaman second. One thing I did learn, though, was that there were other ways of being a quartermaster than going to quartermaster school, or any other rate, for that matter. So I decided I'd still try and be a quartermaster, and I found out there wasn't any more medical problem. Nobody would test my right eye and left eye and all like that. I was in the fleet now and everything was open.

The reason I was in the first division was that the first division handled the ground tackle, and the ship's boatswain and I were the only ones that could splice wire.

Q: That certainly wasn't from your Navy training.

Mr. Bond: No, that was from Herman Larson in the Sea Scouts. I knew my ground tackle and knew about anchors and windlasses. In fact, that schooner I was on had old-fashioned anchors that we fished and catted.

Q: These are the ones with the stocks on them?

Mr. Bond: Yes, and, you know, they were 750-pound anchors. They weren't real heavy, but for a couple of kids to get them in there with a light davit, we had to understand what we were doing.

So, anyway, we went down to the South Pacific. When we crossed the equator, there were so few shellbacks that we had a very easy initiation because they couldn't do much to harass us. We had an advantage of about 90% to 10%. We did get some paddling, and there were a few heads shaved. We got to kiss the baby's belly, and do things like that.

Q: Had you had time to go ashore in Pearl Harbor?

Mr. Bond: Yes, I went ashore several times there, and, of course, the narrow-gauge railway to Honolulu was still running then. Our boat landed us in Pearl City, so we came all the way around from the west there. That was sort of fun, and I often thought that the train now would be the greatest tourist attraction in the world because it went around pretty much the perimeter of the island.

After the war, when my son was Cub Scout age, I was talked into helping take the kids to the transportation museum in Griffith Park in Los Angeles. They had a train ride, and what should I see but the old Oahu Railway. They had the train intact, and I'm sure I had ridden on that train. I rode on the railroad so many times that I must have hit that particular train. I never knew what happened to it until I saw it in the transportation museum in Griffith Park.

Q: How did the liberty atmosphere in Honolulu compare with San Diego?

Mr. Bond: Well, I think Honolulu was a better place to go on liberty. The predominance of servicemen over civilians was really something. In fact, the Honolulu Advertiser, about then or maybe a little bit later, had a reporter stand down on Bishop Street with a counter. He counted 33 servicemen to every civilian that went by.

When you go into Pearl Harbor itself, of course, you come through Kaiwi Channel there and around Diamond Head and just come right across from the Waikiki in Honolulu to Pearl. In those days the Royal Hawaiian Hotel just

Roger Bond #1 - 55

absolutely dominated everything on Waikiki, because there was only the Royal Hawaiian and the Moana, which was a lower, block-style building.

Q: I think the Halekulani was there too.

Mr. Bond: Yes, but it was a little bit farther down. By now the Royal Hawaiian, of course, is just dwarfed by these big hotels. But the beach was open. And, of course, you've got to remember that I was a southern California beach rat in a lot of ways, and I enjoyed going to the beach. As non-rated men, we had to be back aboard ship at 6:00 or something in the evening.*

Q: You talked about the strictness of the drinking age at San Diego. How did it compare in Hawaii?

Mr. Bond: Oh, in Hawaii the qualification was that if you had the price, you got the beer or whatever it was. In the Navy beer gardens and all, people never asked for proof of age. And being brought up in Milwaukee, I always knew what beer tasted like.

Q: Had your buddy Jim Mitchell gone with you to the Saufley?

---

*A non-rated man was an enlisted man who had not been advanced to the rate of petty officer.

Mr. Bond: Oh, I didn't tell you about that. When we left the destroyer base, they said, "Everybody A through L over here, M through Z over there." And that's the last time I saw Jimmy until we were civilians.

Anyway, it was all right. Those were the critical times to have a friend. The cutoff was the funny part, A through L. His last name began with M, so we just missed staying together. Jimmy ended up as a parachute rigger and was always on islands. He knew later on I was on the Saratoga, and a couple of times the Saratoga was in a port where he was stationed. But he couldn't get out to the ship, so we never saw each other in the service after we left San Diego.

Q: How long did the Saufley stay around Hawaii before she headed south?

Mr. Bond: About ten days is all. See, that was in November of '42. The Marines had invaded Guadalcanal the first part of August, and so that part of it was over with. When we got there, things in the Solomons had sort of settled down into a routine of fighting and attrition. The Japanese were still very active. And, of course, the island wasn't really secured for another year.

The way they were working the destroyers was that we were on sort of a three-week rotation, although it wasn't always even weeks. The ship would spend one week up at Guadalcanal or in the Tulagi area. Then we'd go on down to Nouméa, where the tender <u>Dixie</u> was, lay alongside of that, and then go out for convoy duty. When we were up at Guadalcanal, the ship was always on at least Condition II during the daytime. I never ate so many Spam sandwiches in my life.

Q: What does Condition II mean?

Mr. Bond: Well, that's one condition less than general quarters, with full watertight integrity. Condition II has partial integrity. You can open and close doors in order to go through them. About half the crew is on watch, instead of everybody, when there was nothing happening. At night the ship would usually go up and try and cause some trouble. We'd shell a beach or do something. The Japanese were running what we called the Tokyo Express. That was usually several destroyers and a light cruiser or something. They would come down, and, of course, the idea was that we would have to prevent them from getting in and shooting at our people ashore. I went ashore a number of times on working parties and destroyers' parties and that. That was a little bit interesting.

I personally think that Guadalcanal was just as tough a combat campaign as we've ever been in, with the exception of things that were defeats like Bataan, of course, and then the aftermath of Bataan.*

Q: What do you remember from being ashore on those occasions?

Mr. Bond: Well, just like my dad said, it was very muddy. I remember that. The living conditions were bad; it was very humid, very tropical. The equipment really didn't stand up to it: boots, shoes, anything leather was very susceptible to mildew and decay. There was a lot of food problems; a lot of spoilage, things of that sort. It was just a tough darn way to fight a war. The Japanese were very tenacious, and there were no prisoners taken when the Japanese would infiltrate. There were times when the fighter planes taking off from Henderson Field sprayed a few rounds into the brush on the end of the runway, just in case there was anybody there, because there had been so many cases of a sniper getting in there and taking some shots at the planes going out.** It was a tough, tough place.

---

*In late 1941 and early 1942, the Allies suffered heavy casualties and lost many troops to prison camps during operations on the Bataan Peninsula of the island of Luzon in the Philippines.
**Henderson Field was the U.S. airstrip on Guadalcanal.

Q: What did these working parties entail?

Mr. Bond: Well, they were basically stores or ammunition working parties.

Q: The ship was being resupplied?

Mr. Bond: Yes, we'd been drawing supplies or ammunition, mostly ammunition.

Q: Did this experience give you a new appreciation for having a bunk on board ship?

Mr. Bond: Oh, yes, absolutely. I never wanted to transfer to the Marines. Now, Tulagi wasn't so bad. At that time, Tulagi was the administrative headquarters of the Solomons, which meant that there was a town of sorts.

Q: Civilization.

Mr. Bond: Well, not much, but you know, it was a settlement.

One thing that was interesting: a Japanese destroyer had been sunk near Tulagi.* About that time Americans raised that destroyer. It was the most extreme ship I've ever seen to this day in length-to-beam ratio. It was fairly lightly armed, but it was an extremely fast destroyer. The Japanese had a dozen ships of this class, and they used to run our PT boats ashore. The PT boat that had maneuvering room could flat get away from them, but if there was an island in there, the destroyers were fast enough to hem them in where their only escape was to hit the beach.

The destroyer that was salvaged had a well deck in front of the bridge. I saw a triple torpedo mount there, and it had tracks. They could line the mount up on a mark and use the track to reload the torpedoes at sea, which was something we couldn't do. So while they only had a triple mount, they could carry quite a few torpedoes and reload them.

Q: Where were some of the places that you bombarded in those night actions?

---

*The destroyer was the Yayoi of the Mutsuki class; she was sunk by air attack on 9 November 1942. The characteristics for the class: length, 336 feet; beam, 30 feet; maximum draft, 9 feet, 9 inches; displacement, 1,313 tons; speed, 37 knots; main battery, four 4.7-inch guns. The Yayoi was refloated but was too badly damaged for retention. See C. A. Bartholomew, Mud, Muscle, and Miracles (Washington: Department of the Navy, 1990), pages 155-157.

Mr. Bond: Well, I know only part of it, because as I say, I was submerged in the first division. A lot of it was up at the north end of Guadalcanal, went over to Vella Lavella once and Choiseul.

Q: How informed did the captain keep the crew on the ship's mission?

Mr. Bond: Not real well informed. Not names and places, and I guess I'd have to say the crew wasn't as interested in what they were shelling as just the fact that they were doing it. To them it didn't make a damn, and it didn't to me either at that time. I did not have a concept of the Solomons, the layout of it, and the Slot and where Vella Lavella was and Choiseul and New Georgia and then Rendova.

Q: You don't really need to know that in order to load the 5-inch gun.

Mr. Bond: No, that's right. You really don't. The captain would keep us informed as what the duty would be and what to expect. One thing that surprised us was that the Japanese then weren't exploiting the submarines too much. Although they had managed to do a fair amount of damage to warships with the subs, they really used them more as a naval weapon than as a commerce destroyer. As I say, we spent one leg of our tour convoying, and I never heard of any trouble with subs.

Now, one night we were traveling alone after we'd dropped off the merchantman we had been escorting. We were going back home and we did come up on a sub on the surface. And we shot at it and missed, and it dove. We depth-charged it, and we hung around a long time. But with one ship and one sub, it's hard to get a definitive kill. We never were able to claim a kill or anything. That was the only antisubmarine action I saw in the whole war.

Q: Did you have any antiair actions in the <u>Saufley</u>?

Mr. Bond: Not a whole lot; not a whole lot. There was no real concerted combat Japanese action. There was another Japanese deal we called Washing Machine Charlie, who would come over and look at things. Somebody would shoot at him and turn him away.

Q: This was a Japanese plane that would fly over at night?

Mr. Bond: Yes, and generally just seeing what happened but really no air action.

In May of '43 I got sick. I had a real high fever when we were up at Guadalcanal. Then we went down to

Nouméa, and the doctor on the Dixie saw me.* He sent me ashore to the naval hospital, and so then it turned out I had pneumonia.

Q: Although that wasn't the initial diagnosis.

Mr. Bond: No, the initial diagnosis was cat fever, and the medication for that was sweating it out of you.** My chart looked like a small child's pictures of the Alps or something. I lost a tremendous amount of weight from all this perspiration. And one thing I remember, too: cat fever didn't qualify you for any special diet, and I wasn't interested in solid food.

Then one day the doctor was going through. He wasn't even making rounds; he was just going through, and he stopped and looked at that chart. He said, "This man obviously hasn't got this," and went in and ordered me in for an X-ray. By then I was so weak that I could not walk. I think it was shortly after that when I probably gained some weight, and I was still only about 130 pounds. That really was terribly light for me, so I was transferred off the Saufley.

I spent some time there in the hospital. They cured the pneumonia very quickly once it was diagnosed, and it

---
*The USS Dixie (AD-14) was a destroyer tender.
**Catarrhal (known in the Navy as "cat") fever is an inflammation of the mucous membranes, especially those involving the nose and air passages.

was with sulfa. Then it was mostly a case of getting my strength back. As soon as I got a little strength, I started running because I had run track in school. I remember one day the guys asked me if I wanted to join a basketball game. My whole shooting rhythm was way off, and my shots were all falling short because I didn't have the strength.

While I was at the receiving station there, I don't know how it came about, but about eight or ten men were transferred out to the Saratoga.*

Q: What month was that?

Mr. Bond: That was on June 14, 1943. It didn't seem like the Saratoga expected us or wanted any men. They put us in the 19th division, which was sort of a labor gang under the master-at-arms until we were put into some sort of a billet.

I remember one thing we did when the carrier went into port. The air group usually left and went to a field before the ship went into port, so we had only a couple of planes left aboard. One of our jobs one day was to paint the flight deck. When somebody tells you you're going to

---

*The USS Saratoga (CV-3) was commissioned 16 November 1927 In World War II she had a standard displacement of 37,700 tons, was 888 feet long, 106 feet in the beam, an extreme width of 130 feet on the flight deck, and had a draft of 24 feet. She had a top speed of 33.5 knots and could accommodate approximately 60-70 aircraft.

paint the flight deck, and you stand on a flight deck that's more than 900 feet long and roughly 130 feet wide, it's pretty hard to believe that you're going to do it in one day. I was on the painting crew, and some of the other guys were on the carrying crew. We painted that flight deck with swabs. It was what I call a gray whitewash or grayish blue, and, by gosh, we got it painted by 4:00 o'clock.

Q: By whitewash do you mean it wasn't the consistency of paint?

Mr. Bond: No, it was a thin thing, and, of course, the deck was teak, and it soaked it in pretty well. It wouldn't have done to paint metal. I found out that they painted the flight deck every couple of months when the planes weren't on it. They told me it didn't do it any good to paint it with good paint because the wheels and the skidding would just wear it off. This worked as well as quality paint.

But, anyway, as I did on the <u>Saufley</u>, I said I wanted to be a quartermaster. When you're in this position, you don't know how the communication travels if you tell somebody something like that. I said it to a master-at-arms, but he was in charge of us and he passed it on. Then the navigator called me down to his navigation office and, as I said, asked me if I knew anything about optics and what courses I'd taken in school and all. He was a fellow by the name of Robert Beebe, who lived in Annapolis, Maryland, and was a great advocate of the "sharpy" sailboat.*

Q: Was he an aviator?

Mr. Bond: Yes, he was, but he never did any flying duty on the ship. I think he was an aviator for purposes of career and not because he was really interested in aviation and wanted to fly.

Q: Was that something you picked up from talking to him, or how did you get that impression?

Mr. Bond: Well, it's more from the fact that he didn't have a lot of interest in flying. You didn't hear him conversing about flying with pilots. I contrast him to several other officers that were primarily fliers that were just doing duty in a non-flying way.

Q: Ship's company.

---
*Lieutenant Commander Robert P. Beebe, USN.

Mr. Bond: Yes, like the air officer, for instance, flight deck officer, and the landing signal officer. They weren't in flying billets, but they'd fly every chance they had. Beebe didn't do that. There were a lot of officers, in the late '30s especially, that began to see that being a flier opened up career opportunities to them, and so they became qualified. Of course, the main career opportunity was to be a carrier captain or an admiral. But Beebe was a fine man. He was a nice guy and good officer.

The navigation division of that ship was very small. We had a chief quartermaster, two firsts, two seconds, three thirds, three strikers, and a yeoman.* Then we had the two chaplain's yeomen; I guess that's navigation of a different sort. They had to put them someplace. It was just a very small group. And the commander didn't use a lot of military discipline or anything like that, especially in port.

We had to maintain the whole issue of the Hydrographic Office and charts. The first class and the chief always stood charthouse watches under way. Altogether we had eight watch standers: three strikers, three thirds, and two seconds. That let us have two quartermasters on watch at all times under way. One was in steering aft, and one was in the pilothouse as quartermaster of the watch. When

---
*A striker is a non-rated enlisted man officially designated as being in training for a specific rating.

we were in port we only had one on duty at a time on the quarterdeck. That was when we had to do most of our chart work, because you couldn't do much of it under way.* The charthouse was too small to do that. So we would be up there working, and each quartermaster had certain portfolios of charts that he took care of. Commander Beebe would be working there or reading in there, doing something, and he'd be around us. It was a very informal, easy association.

The thing that was amazing about my work with the quartermasters was that it just really changed my whole naval awareness. All of a sudden, now I was in a position that I was aware of a lot of different functions of the ship. I was in the nerve center of the ship, you might say. I kept contact with all different branches of the ship, interacted with them, knew what was going on, where we were going, how we were getting there, and all that sort of thing. It was just completely different situation from being immersed in the first division of the Saufley.

Q: So that the pneumonia was a well disguised blessing.

Mr. Bond: It surely was, it surely was.

I've always liked maps, so I love charts. Now I was

---

*After they are printed initially, navigation charts are subsequently updated by hand, incorporating information sent to each chart holder by the Navy Hydrographic Office.

picking up again on a lot of things I'd been involved with in just seamanship from before and doing things that I'd looked forward to do. For example, I was really aware of things like compensating compasses. Those were things that I knew about and helped do in civilian life, and now I was back doing those kinds of things. I'll tell you one thing, to compensate a magnetic compass in an off-center aircraft carrier is really a chore.

Q: How do you go about doing it?

Mr. Bond: Well, you know, you have what we call navigator's balls. These are large iron balls that are adjusted in position to take care of the one kind of deviation caused by the earth's magnetic field. There's also a flinders bar in front of the binnacle that takes care of the vertical deviation. You put different amounts of magnets in there. To do this compensation you have to swing the ship, and you're constantly trying to take out the error--the deviation in the ship--halving it and halving it and trying to bring it down. But since the compass is off-center, on the side in the island structure, it's very hard to get it real close. And, of course, if you get too many magnets, all of a sudden the compass card just swings free. You've overpowered the earth's magnetism, and then it doesn't work. But, anyway, that sort of thing was exciting stuff for us.

Beebe had a very inquiring mind. He was interested in tides and currents. Like we'd be in a certain port, although this didn't apply to Nouméa, because there wasn't any tide in Nouméa to speak of. But later on, when we were up in the New Hebrides and Espiritu Santo, at the main fleet base there was a channel, Segond Channel, and it had quite a tidal current in it. There wasn't anything in the sailing directions about it, so Beebe decided we would contribute. We studied the tides and took readings on the velocity every hour and when they shifted. But that was a lot of fun to do things like that. That was the kind of thing that I had envisioned myself doing in the merchant marine or whatever; it was real seamanship type of work.

Q: And it was certainly more challenging mentally than loading a 5-inch gun.

Mr. Bond: That's right, or just taking care of it. Although I did do some gunnery work. I got to know a couple of gunner's mates who lived in the compartment next to ours. Shatsnider was one of them, and he was a damn good gunner's mate.* Every once in a while, I'd go up and help him tear down a 5-inch gun just for the fun of it.

---
*Gunner's Mate Second Class Robert C. Shatsnider.

It was a beautiful hunk of machinery, all the cam work and everything in it.

But I enjoyed the quartermaster work and the navigation work. Commander Beebe, the chief, and everybody were always glad somebody learned navigation. I mean, the ship wasn't going to depend on me, but they felt that was a worthwhile activity, and anybody that wanted to work sights and all that, it was great as far as they were concerned.* Nobody held you back. We'd take sun lines in the morning and the afternoon--just part of the regular quartermaster of the watch work. And that was always fun. Then, of course, I was always preparing myself to get back on destroyers, so I kept in touch with the visual signaling as much as I could. It was very close--about four steps from the navigation bridge to the signal bridge.

Q: Did you feel any sense of disadvantage in not having gone to the formal quartermaster school?

Mr. Bond: No, in fact, I decided later on that it was almost an advantage.

Q: In what sense?

---

*In celestial navigation, individuals take sights of the angle above the horizon for various heavenly bodies. These angles are then used with a nautical almanac to compute lines of position on a chart. Where the lines of position intersect is the ship's position at the time of the sights.

Mr. Bond: I guess it was because the quartermaster school was taught in generalities and taught by people who were quite a bit removed from actual sea experience. When you get in something like that, and you're straight out of boot camp, it's very hard for you to sort out what's really useful and what's sort of academic.

Q: Well, and you have to use so much imagination too.

Mr. Bond: Yes. I know I talked to a number of men that'd gone through officer training, and especially people that came from non-maritime areas. Looking back, they felt there was a lot of useful material thrown at them, but they didn't sort it out right.

Q: Well, and it's also conceptual instead of practical.

Mr. Bond: Yes, but I will say that that was a really outstanding group of men in that quartermaster division. So I can't visualize me being in school with teachers as good as the men in that division. And the class was very small; it was basically just a couple of us, you know.

Q: The other advantage is that you can apply things right away.

Mr. Bond: Right. And the chief was a fellow that had been in the Navy 19 years when I came aboard; Willard Gain was his name.* He was from upstate Wisconsin. He had joined the Navy in the mid-1920s, and he went out to China when he was 18. They weren't supposed to send 18-year-olds out, but some way he talked his way out there. He'd spent a lot of time out in the Asiatic Fleet and in China. He was a very good quartermaster, but he'd had quite a career of deck and summary court-martials and probably never would have made chief if it hadn't been for the war. But that was his riotous youth and all. He knew what he was doing. He had spent about three years on a tanker. I really got the feeling that the navigator of the tanker just let Gain navigate the ship because he was good at it, and liked to do it, and so he basically did it. And, of course, a tanker moves around a lot, so he got a lot of active work.

Then we had a first class named Smith from Oklahoma, who had about nine years in the Navy.** Had another first class, name of Willie Hart.*** He was the one from Versailles, [pronounced Ver-sales] Missouri. By the way, a humorous story was that somebody saw one of his letters and said, "I didn't know there was a Versailles [pronounced Ver-sigh] in Missouri."

---
*Chief Quartermaster Willard M. Gain, USN.
**Quartermaster First Class Robert E. Smith, USN.
***Quartermaster First Class William H. Hart, USN.

Willie said, "Only you and the librarian think there is."

Willie hadn't been in the Navy too long, probably only about four or five years, but he was a very, very sharp guy. With the educational opportunities nowadays, these guys wouldn't be enlisted men in the Navy. They would have been doing something else.

Q: Well, they had enlisted during the Depression.

Mr. Bond: That's right. And then we had a second class by the name of Black, who had been on the Nevada at Pearl Harbor. In fact, he was the lee helmsman when they were making their break for the open water. The chief told them to put the helm over and they beached her. He had about eight or nine years in the Navy.

The other second class was a fellow by the name of Les Shryer.* Now, he came in 1940. He was a little bit older, and he was well-educated. He worked for the Santa Fe Railway in the right-of-way department in that division between Gallup, New Mexico, and Barstow, California. One of the things about that is they had a contract with the Navajo nation, and the Navajo furnished labor for the railroad. He was the only white man I know that spoke Navajo. Les was a very intelligent guy.

---

*Quartermaster Second Class Leslie S. Shryer, USN.

Then the third class: we had one from Chicago, Fritz Martin Kirsch, who was a German-born boy. His two brothers were in the Marines and he was in the Navy. And Fritz was a peacetime sailor, too, about three years, I guess. Then we had a third class by the name of Campbell who had 12 years in the Navy. The only trouble Campbell had was that he could never go on an overnight liberty. When he left, somebody had to go get him. He was a tremendous quartermaster. I mean, when he was on watch, he'd take over the ship if the officer of the deck would let him, and he was just great. He got transferred. Somebody ran into him a couple years later, or less than that, and he was already a chief. As long as he wasn't around where he could get into trouble by going on liberty, his natural ability was such that he went right up.

Q: So you were really the new kid on the block with all this talent.

Mr. Bond: You bet, and, you know, to be a slick-armed quartermaster was really something.

Q: What do you mean by that term?

Mr. Bond: No hash marks.* But they were great teachers.

---

*A hash mark is the nickname for a diagonal service stripe worn on the left sleeve of an enlisted man's jumper or

We lived in this one little berthing compartment. Then we had a storeroom up in the bow, the anchor windlass area, where we kept all the flags, kept all the clocks, and had a sewing machine to repair flags. Two quartermasters lived up there for three months at a time, and that was their cleaning station. The rest of us slept back in the main compartment, which was C-0107-L. The C meant it was in the C portion of the ship, 01 being the deck and 07 being fourth compartment back from the C bulkhead on the starboard side, L for living space.

We played a lot of cards. These were intelligent men; they were good card players; and pinochle was the favorite game in that compartment, and a lot of good conversation. They had been on a lot of different ships and seen a lot of different duties.

Q: Were those the two main forms of recreation, card playing and talking?

Mr. Bond: Yes, I would say that.

In most ports you went into in those days they'd have a recreation beach. The ship carried beer, and you'd go ashore and they'd take the ship's beer ashore. You'd have chits for a couple of cans of beer. That was the basic recreation even in Nouméa. Nouméa was a town, but this was a French community that was drawn in on itself, and there was no penetration there. They weren't interested in fleecing the sailors or anything else. So the only man I knew that ever really got along was a kid whose family was French Canadian, and he spoke French. He went to the Catholic priest there and asked if he couldn't serve as an altar boy. The priest was so delighted to have this boy. Of course, the sailor's purposes were strictly long range, but he was then introduced by the priest to several people who then accepted him. So he liked Nouméa.

Q: What sort of people did he get introduced to?

Mr. Bond: Oh, nothing sensational. He did get to meet some families and spend some time with them, and I think he went to some social events. He liked Nouméa. But for the rest of us, we never really spent time ashore because there were an awful lot of ships in the harbor and servicemen on the island.

Q: Were there rivalries between different ships?

Mr. Bond: Yes, and I would say the rivalry between the Saratoga and the Enterprise was almost as great as the rivalry between the Americans and the Japanese.

Q: How did that manifest itself?

Mr. Bond: Well, mostly jealousy.

Q: Were there fights or name-calling?

Mr. Bond: Oh, you know, two beers and a wrong word, and there'd be a fight. They just tried to generally keep the two crews apart. But then the Enterprise didn't spend a whole lot of time in the same port with the Saratoga. After I came aboard it was doing duty elsewhere. This period in the summer and fall of '43 was a lull time when both the Japanese and the Americans were sort of taking stock and building up our forces. Both sides had lost quite a bit. When I was down there on the Saufley in late '42 and early '43, we were still afraid we were losing the war in the South Pacific. We had this feeling that we were holding the Japanese back, but if anything unlucky happened, like losing one of the important ships, why, then the balance would be tipped.

Q: In '42 we lost the Lexington, Yorktown, Hornet, and Wasp. We didn't have too many carriers to spare.

Mr. Bond: No, that's right. And, you know, in the Saratoga we felt we were the only ones. We didn't know what the hell happened to the Enterprise. We knew the

Ranger was on the East Coast, but we just felt that we were the only ones. The British sent the carrier HMS Victorious out for the New Georgia campaign. We operated with them. That was sort of fun. The Victorious was a pretty good carrier; I'd say it was about Wasp's size.* It was a pretty slick-looking ship, and they were fine to operate with.

I remember one story that I read later on in The Reader's Digest, one of those little quips at the end. The British weren't used to staying out at sea quite as long as the Americans. When we were furnishing air cover, for instance, we might stay out about 30 days. After a while the British started running low on potatoes, so we loaded up a torpedo plane with dehydrated potatoes and sent it over to them. We got this message back: "We've fried them; we've baked them; we've broiled them. How the hell do you cook them?" So they sent a cook over to show them how to prepare dehydrated potatoes. I don't know that we were doing them any great favor, though.

One thing about the Saratoga was that the crew was quite a bit larger than they had anticipated the wartime complement would be. The ship just did not have enough

---

*HMS Victorious was completed in May 1941. She was 753 feet long overall, had a standard displacement of 23,000 tons, and carried 33 aircraft. The USS Wasp (CV-7) was commissioned 25 April 1940. She was 741 feet long, had a standard displacement of 14,700 tons, and could accommodate approximately 80 aircraft. The Wasp was sunk 15 September 1942 while supporting the Guadalcanal operation.

storage space for food. In the '20s, when it was designed, they didn't think in terms of enough refrigerated storage space. When we'd go to sea, they would have food stacked in the passageways. There'd always be things like onions, for instance.

Q: Not anything men wanted to pilfer.

Mr. Bond: Not desirable, no. And, boy, I'm glad I was never a seaman or fireman on that ship, because I avoided getting assigned to the "breakout gang." The breakout gang on the <u>Saratoga</u> started way down in those storerooms. They had to come up at least five, six decks to the mess hall and the galleys on the main deck, immediately under the flight deck. So a man had to put a case of lettuce or something on his shoulder and just go up, up, up, up, up. That was nothing but hard labor. Those were little things that showed you that it was a ship of the old Navy. They had more hard-labor routines on older ships than they did on new ships.

Q: Could you describe the living arrangements on board? Those dated from an earlier era also.

Mr. Bond: Yes, that's right. Well, right till the end, they had about 700 men sleeping in hammocks in the mess halls. Now, that was not as bad a deal as it could have been, because when those hammocks were stowed, you had big, open mess halls. All the tables were stowed in racks under the overhead, and so were the hammocks, and there was just a clear deck. I know at times at night you'd be going through there; maybe you were on the morning watch and you had calls to make.* You saw all these humps hanging down, so you had to sort of duck-walk to get under them. Sometimes, all of a sudden you'd hear, THUMP! and "Goddammit." Then some guy picked himself off the deck and crawled back in his hammock. He had fallen out of one of those "humps."

Q: Was that an art, learning how to sleep in a hammock, or did you ever have to do that?

Mr. Bond: Well, the only time I ever did was when I wanted to, and it wasn't so difficult. With all the guys sleeping there, one or two was bound to fall out, but you didn't want to turn over. I think what got you in trouble was hanging your arms or legs out. That destroyed your balance, made you a little more tippy, and that's why you fell out. It'd come up on the side of you when you were in it.

In the hot weather the hammock could be a little bit

---
*Officially the morning watch ran from 0400 to 0800. In practice it was began at 0345 and was relieved at 0715.

stifling. You've heard of radiant heat in houses, where it comes up from the floor. Here you were right under the flight deck, which sent down radiant heat from above. That dark gray deck was soaking up heat all day long and radiating it down.

Aside from the spaces with guys sleeping in hammocks, the other compartments were what I'd call pretty straightforward naval compartments. The Saratoga's hangar deck did not go from one end of the ship to the other. I don't know what the thinking was, but it went from pretty far aft to about even with the bridge structure.

Q: Airplanes were pretty small when she was designed.

Mr. Bond: Right, and somehow they didn't seem to think it was important to be able to warm up planes on the hangar deck. Also, the hangar deck did not extend to the outside of the ship. Now, our compartment was a wing compartment between the hangar deck and the outside hull. All these compartments had a characteristic of being long and narrow.

Most people have seen pictures of Saratoga; among the outstanding characteristics were the boat pockets on the sides of the ship. There were three on the port side and one on the starboard side. Our compartment was just aft of the starboard boat pocket. In peacetime those boat pockets were used to store the motor launches. We had a couple of 50-footers, two 40s, a 36, and a couple of motor whaleboats. But, see, those boat pockets illustrated the fact that the hangar deck did not come out to the side, and that's about how wide the compartments were.

So that was a peculiarity, and another peculiarity was that your compartment was also a passageway. The way you got from one compartment to another was going through one in between, and they'd be in a whole series.

Q: Did you have regular bunks in your compartment?

Mr. Bond: Yes. We had the bunks against both fore-and-aft bulkheads, and the lockers were in the middle. Just before I came aboard, they had foot lockers, and that made it a little more open in the center of the compartment. On the other hand, it gave them less room in the bunks because they had three bunks above the foot locker in less space. The guys felt this new way was a lot better.

There were no wash basins or anything like that. Each man had a bucket and he'd draw his water--cold water--and then take it to a steam jet. He stuck the jet in and heated the water to whatever temperature he wanted. Then he would soap himself down from that and then get into a cold shower to rinse off.

One thing I always wondered about--but never wanted to

find out from personal experience--was what would happen if the ship ever operated in the Aleutians. It just seemed to me that cold weather would have created a really complicated life because of the way it was set up.

Q: What was the head like? It had these cold showers you've described. What else?

Mr. Bond: We had three big washrooms, and at any given time one of them was usually shut down for cleaning. Then the heads themselves were troughs that had water flowing through them. Where they were used as urinals, of course, there'd be no divisions. On the ones that were used for bowel movements, you'd have two boards on the trough. And then the stream ran through and then out the sides of the ship; in port, at sea, that's the way it was.

Q: Were there wash basins in the washroom?

Mr. Bond: No, not at all. That's what your bucket was for--to use as a wash basin.

Q: Did that include brushing teeth and shaving?

Mr. Bond: Yes.

Q: Did they have mirrors for the shaving?

Mr. Bond: Yes, they had mirrors. They didn't want you to hurt yourself. The first thing you did in the routine was brush your teeth when the water was clean. Then you shaved, and then you sort of washed down. If you had to wash any clothes, you'd wash them in what was left of the water.

Q: Was there a limit on how much fresh water you could draw?

Mr. Bond: We never had a limit, because the crew was very good. The only time we ever got into any problem was when we were carrying passengers and overloaded the system. But that was a remarkable thing, that the crew was mindful of the water. Of course, what helped was the showers were cold, and with the buckets you just didn't tend to waste it. If you were caught wasting water, you were put on a list. When it came time to scale the evaporators, the men on the list were part of the work crew, and that was, I understand, a very nasty job, especially in the tropics. There wasn't much ventilation, so it was a hot job that meant working with that salt and getting salt all over you.

Q: Sort of like at boot camp having the company march

across your clothes. You didn't make that mistake more than once.

Mr. Bond: That's right. Hardly anybody did serve twice.

Q: Well, wasn't this sort of a setback from the living conditions in the modern <u>Saufley</u>?

Mr. Bond: Yes, but, of course, a tin can's awfully crowded.* The engine space on a destroyer takes up an inordinate amount of room compared to a larger ship like the <u>Saratoga</u>. And, of course, the engines of the <u>Saratoga</u> were buried deep. In the <u>Saufley</u> the engineering space came right up to the main deck, so berthing compartments were really split fore and aft of that.

Q: But you didn't have to live out of a bucket, though, did you?

Mr. Bond: No, no, that sort of thing you didn't. The washrooms were fine. It was just like ashore.

Q: Where did you eat in the <u>Saratoga</u>?

---

*"Tin can" is a long-time Navy slang term for a destroyer. It derives from the relatively thin hull plating of a destroyer when compared to larger armored ships such as cruisers and battleships. An even shorter version of the term is "can," which Bond uses later in the oral history.

Mr. Bond: Well, the mess deck was a deck right under the hangar deck where all the men in hammocks lived. The mess tables were stored in racks in the overhead when they weren't being used. They were rigged for meals when the hammocks were put away. For the first four or five months I was aboard, we had table mess. That was where you sat down as a division. Larger divisions pretty much ate by sections, and the senior man ate at the head of the table. When the mess cook brought the meat, it went to him first, and then it came down to you at the foot of the table. I never did get a piece of meat that was bigger than a quarter. I mean, I got a lot of meat but no one piece was ever very big. I'll eat almost anything, and so when there were certain things that most of the guys didn't like, then I ate quite a bit.

Q: Such as?

Mr. Bond: Well, remarkably, spareribs. I couldn't believe that everybody didn't love spareribs. I remember one time I had 56 of them in one meal. They were small, and you've got to remember, I was getting my strength back too.

Q: Oh, yes.

Mr. Bond: I was underweight when I went aboard ship, and so I ate everything that I could reach. After those first four months we changed to the cafeteria system of serving, and everyone had equal chance for the better cuts of meat.

Q: What did dehydrated potatoes taste like once they were prepared?

Mr. Bond: They were always mashed, and they were sort of gray. And then they varied in consistency with how carefully the cooks mixed them. If they didn't get enough moisture in, they were really pretty pasty. But you could put a lot of pepper on, and then you could eat them. One time we were out of port 87 straight days, and we were getting down to a very poor selection of food. There was one heck of a lot of beans and rice. Until you got to that point, when you still had variety, you could tell what day of the week it was by what you ate for breakfast.

I remember when I was home on leave and the family was there, including my aunts and my mother. I was telling about this rotation of items on the breakfast menu, and one day it was chipped beef on toast. But I didn't know what chipped beef on toast was actually called. I was going along, and when I got to that, I just stopped dead. I didn't know how to describe it except "shit on a shingle." I said, "Well, it's just sort of a messy thing on toast."

When I got back to the ship, I had to find out what it really was because I might be called upon to say it again. That's when I found out it was chipped beef on toast.

Q: Well, a typical Saturday morning meal, I guess, was cornbread and beans.

Mr. Bond: Right, that was Saturday morning and Sunday supper it was beans too.

Q: How much sleep could you get in a wartime situation like that?

Mr. Bond: Well, I've never had much trouble keeping irregular hours. I think a lot of it comes from attitude, because since I was a teenager I had assumed that I would be doing sea duty. Whenever you're going to do sea duty, you're going to get involved in watches. So to me it seemed perfectly normal.

Now, this is a variation of what Herman Larson said when I was too old to go to sea, that I was used to comforts ashore, and one of them is sleeping through the night. But I never had any trouble varying my sleeping time and standing watches and getting up for the midwatch. But I had to know that I was getting up for the midwatch. One night the man that was supposed to have the midwatch turned in to sick bay after I'd gone to bed. I was the next guy on the list, and so they tried to wake me up for the midwatch. They had a heck of a time waking me up.

Normally if I had the watch, all you had to do was touch the bunk and say my name and I was awake. If you had the midwatch and you were in a normal routine, you could sleep in for another hour past reveille. Even the guys in hammocks could do that. So I never felt that I was ever having a problem with sleep. And another thing, I could sleep almost anywhere. When we were a long time at general quarters and in security condition II and all, they asked you not to leave your stations. Obviously you're not going to go sit in the corner of the pilothouse and go to sleep, but I could go back to the signal bridge or back to secondary control and just crap out. We'd usually go back there because there was a catwalk from the bridge structure back to the stack structure, and around secondary control another bridge was back there. We had a conning tower, too--the only carrier with a conning tower.

Q: Where was that?

Mr. Bond: That was immediately below the bridge. Of course, that was for when the ship was going to operate as

Roger Bond #1 - 91

a heavy cruiser, with 8-inch guns.*

Q: Well, you're saying the only one, that's because the Lexington had been sunk.**

Mr. Bond: Yes, the "Lex" was identical. But you could go down and sleep there, and the quartermasters were the only ones that ever went in there. We kept it clean, but they very, very seldom ever took steering control or anything like that in the conning tower.

Q: Were you surprised by how small the bridge structure was in such a large ship?

Mr. Bond: No, I was aware that it would be, but one thing that surprised me was the fact that we had so much work to do in such a small space.

Q: Were you on top of each other frequently?

Mr. Bond: Yes, the pilothouse was a pretty crowded place. It was maybe about 25 by 20 feet. You had a helmsman, you

---

*The Saratoga had originally been planned as a battle cruiser. She was converted during construction in the 1920s but still given the armament of a heavy cruiser. She was originally outfitted with eight 8-inch guns in four turrets. The turrets were removed in 1942 to make room for dual-purpose 5-inch/38 gun mounts.
**The Saratoga's sister ship, the USS Lexington (CV-2) was sunk on 8 May 1942 during the Battle of the Coral Sea.

had a lee helmsman, and a couple of telephone talkers. You had a quartermaster of the watch and his desk, a Marine time orderly during the day, and a boatswain's mate of the watch. During the day you had a bugler. In charge of all these men was the officer of the deck, and then when we got so many officers, we had a junior officer of the deck, and sometimes the captain would even squeeze in too.

Q: What was the function of the Marine time orderly?

Mr. Bond: Well, I'll be darned if I know why we needed him, but he was basically the officer of the deck's orderly. Also, he'd tell you when it was time to have a bugler blow mess call or something like that. He was following the plan of the day. And that ship was really great on bugle calls. They even had a Marine bugler. We did just about everything by bugle calls.

Q: So that the word was not passed orally very much?

Mr. Bond: Well, not if they could possibly do it with a bugle call, or boatswain's call.

Q: So after a while you gradually learned what all of these were.

Mr. Bond: Yes, you did. And, of course, we had words for some of them. For mail call it was, "I got a letter, I got a letter, you got a postcard."

Q: It take it the words fit the rhythm of the bugle call.

Mr. Bond: Yes.

Q: How important was mail to the men of a ship at sea?

Mr. Bond: Well, it was pretty important. We didn't get a lot of it. There wasn't a steady supply because we moved a lot, and you didn't get mail while you were at sea. You'd get it in port. We'd go out on these exercises that lasted 30, 40 days. Now, we'd usually leave a couple of mail clerks behind, and they'd sort mail while we were gone. So when we got back in, usually the mail boat was alongside about the time we dropped anchor. But it all came aboard sorted, and it was pretty important.

Q: Did you have much chance to write letters?

Mr. Bond: Oh, yes, you could write letters day by day. Some guys wrote a lot, especially the newlyweds. They wrote to their wives every day. I sort of wrote letters when I got letters. And, of course, all the letters went through censorship, which was done with a scissors. The officers cut out the things you weren't supposed to write. Guys that didn't know what to say cut up their own letters, pretending that the officers did the censoring. The person they were writing to got this letter full of holes and thought, "Gee, he must have had a lot of interesting things to say."

Q: So it was sort of a gag.

Mr. Bond: Well, they'd just blame it on the fact that the censor cut it out.

Q: Were you briefed on what you should and shouldn't say?

Mr. Bond: Oh, yes. You couldn't say whether you were at sea or in port, whether it was hot or cold, or where we were at or anything like that or you'd seen any action. That's why it really became difficult to say things and write an interesting letter. You could reminisce, you could look ahead, you could look behind, but you couldn't dwell on the present too much.

I can mention some other things on the living conditions there. The brig was brutal. I never was in it, but I never wanted to be in it. The cells were four by four feet; the doors were lattice work of steel bands with the open basket weave.

Q: So you couldn't lie down.

Mr. Bond: You couldn't really lie down. And there was no bunk in the cell. You slept on the deck; you brought your blanket. When they said ten days on bread and water, they really meant it. A prisoner got a full ration every three days, and, of course, there were Marine guards. In the daytime the prisoners had to stand; there was no talking. If a man leaned on the bulkheads or the door or something, they'd give him an extra day. But there were a lot of guys on that ship that if it wasn't that way, they'd rather spend the time in the brig than chipping paint, or breakout gang, or something like that.

After July we moved the <u>Saratoga</u> from Nouméa up to the island of Efate, in the New Hebrides. The harbor there had absolutely no habitation on it as far as I know. It was a very deep harbor; we continually anchored in 30 fathoms. But do you know, the water was so clear that if you followed the chain down with your eye, you could see that anchor in 30 fathoms. We'd put out 160, 170 fathoms of chain. And you'd also sail the <u>Saratoga</u> so close to the beach that you could swear you could throw a rock ashore. The water was deep immediately.

At that time the Idaho and the Mississippi were operating with us. A little carrier, the Breton, a CVE, operated there.* It was the only CVE I was ever around that actually operated aircraft. When they operated with us, we went up to Rendova.

Q: Do you have any recollections of those operations with the battleships?

Mr. Bond: No, they just sort of tagged along. And then at Rendova they went in and shelled the beach.

Q: Did you provide air cover for them?

Mr. Bond: Right, we were providing air cover for that and the beachhead when in operations like that. We basically operated an 84-plane air group. When we'd get into a support situation like that, the Saratoga just had planes over the target all day. These were small sorties, and they'd be coming and going. And I think that the Breton operated 18 torpedo planes; that's all they did.

Q: That's an unusual air group.

---

*CVEs were escort carriers that could operate aircraft but were slower, smaller, and less capable than the attack carriers. Often they were used to ferry aircraft or in combat roles that did not require much speed.

Mr. Bond: Right.

Earlier, you asked about homosexuality. While we were at Efate, we had four general court-martials aboard the Saratoga. I think one was a crewman of the Saratoga.

One general court-martial was for a commander who was the supply officer of the Saratoga. He was caught up by the IRS from prewar deals and kickbacks and procuring food in Long Beach.* I guess the IRS was onto the people that he was doing business with and it unraveled and implicated him. But the other three were for homosexual acts. I cannot really say if they were homosexual people involved. The indictments were for committing sodomy, but I believe the guilty parties were probably heterosexual. This could be compared to prison rape.

I guess I was a very naive person, but I think a lot of people were in those days.

Q: Well, it wasn't discussed openly in the news media the way it is today.

Mr. Bond: No, that's right. It was, you know, really shocking to me, and, of course, in that atmosphere I can see why the Navy just could not tolerate anything approaching that because, there we were in the tropics. Here you were down in your compartment and you decided to

---
*IRS--Internal Revenue Service.

shower and shave, do a little laundry. You took off your clothes, and you undid your underwear. You had only three or four suits of underwear, so you took them off and you put them all in the bucket. Then you walked up to the washrooms basically naked.

During the whole time in the washroom, while you were scrubbing your clothes and showering, everybody could see you. These were open showers with no partitions or anything of any sort. I mean, just over along that bulkhead there were a couple of showers, and the whole thing's tiled. Essentially, the whole compartment was one big shower, you might say. I don't believe you can have a homosexual in a situation like that. It isn't a matter of any level of sophistication or anything else; it just can't be in that situation. It would be like turning a guy loose in nurses' quarters; he'd just be continually aroused. It was really a shocking situation.

But it was also very interesting. The general court-martial was held in the library, which was pretty good size. The officers on the courts were from the various ships, and they'd come aboard in dress whites and usually with swords. When the court convened, the Saratoga fired a gun and put the union jack at the starboard yardarm.*

---

*The union jack is a small flag that amounts to a portion of a U.S. national flag--the part with white stars on a blue background. It is typically flown from a jackstaff on the bow of a Navy ship when she is moored or anchored.

Every damn person in that harbor knew what was going on. When the findings came out, they were read at quarters to everybody in that command. I really felt sorry for that commander with the IRS problems.

Q: Why?

Mr. Bond: Well, he'd destroyed himself. I didn't condone it or anything, but when they read that sentence out loud, it was a public humiliation. The sentence called for him to be transferred to the naval disciplinary barracks at Portsmouth for 20 years, reduced to apprentice seaman, and dismissed from the service. It was a very dramatic thing.

Q: Well, if that sentence really was executed that way, he didn't get out until Kennedy was President.*

Mr. Bond: That's right. But I imagine, like most prison sentences, he would get time off for good behavior. And he undoubtedly was going to be on good behavior. He wasn't a violent person.

Well, I've been active a little bit through a church ministry at Sandstone Federal Prison up towards Duluth, Minnesota. One of the things that strikes me is there isn't a lot of difference between those guys inside and

---

*John F. Kennedy was President of the United States from January 1961 to November 1963.

people outside. They just got a little variance and got in some illegal activities. Now, federal prisons deal with more non-violent type of stuff, so you get embezzlers and smugglers and things of that sort.

Q: I have a feeling, though, that there were some enlisted men in the crew who probably were delighted that an officer got publicly humiliated.

Mr. Bond: Oh, I'm sure that's true, but I think he was a fairly well liked officer before this came up. I think he felt temptation, and probably the kickback was offered, and he had the weakness not to refuse it. But it was a very sobering experience for a young man.

Q: And meant to be so, I'm sure.

Mr. Bond: Absolutely. Sure, that's why they go through all the things like that and fire the gun. Of course, when the court was adjourned, they fired the gun again and then took down the jack. Being a quartermaster, I was involved. We were the guys that put the jack up and took care of that part of it. Another thing was that everything that happened on that ship, we logged in the quartermaster's notebook. So you were very aware of all these things going on, and the seriousness of it.

We didn't stay at Efate too long. I think we only went in and out of there a couple times. That's where Captain Mullinnix was transferred; he made rear admiral.*

Q: Do you have any recollections of him individually before he left?

Mr. Bond: He was a very quiet, scholarly man. Before him was Captain Bogan, whom I really didn't know personally.** But I felt that I did, because I heard so many stories about him. He had left just shortly before I came aboard. Bogan was a hard drinker and a hard fighter. He had been a boxer at the Naval Academy and all that sort of thing. Bogan had a reputation that if you came up to mast before him for anything involving drinking, there'd be no mercy, because he handled himself and expected you to.

Mullinnix was a teetotaler. He looked upon drinking as a weakness or a disease, and he would be very tolerant. I mean, he didn't approve of misdeeds, so you paid for them, but you didn't pay hard. With Bogan it was three days' bread and water right now if anything you did, such as being late, was caused by drinking. That was always an interesting thing--that a non-drinker was much more gentle

---
*Captain Henry M. Mullinnix, USN, was commanding officer of the Saratoga from April to August of 1943.
**Captain Gerald F. Bogan, USN, commanded the ship from October 1942 to March 1943. The oral history of Bogan, a retired vice admiral, is in the Naval Institute collection.

than a drinker. Mullinnix was really well liked by the crew. And, of course, he took his flag to the Liscome Bay, which was torpedoed off Tarawa, and that was the end of him.* When Mullinnix left, John Cassady came aboard.** Cassady was aboard then until we were in Bremerton the following year.

Q: You told me a story the other night about Captain Bogan that bears repeating. It was about his promotion of an enlisted man.

Mr. Bond: Yes, that was at the club in Nouméa. He'd had quite a bit to drink, and he challenged anybody in the place to a fight. There was one man named Derry who was drunk enough to take him up on it.*** Of course, Bogan wasn't near the fighter he used to be, and Derry just floored him, knocked him cold. The next day the word was passed, "Gunner's Mate First Class Derry report to the captain's cabin."

Derry told us later that when he went in, the captain said, "Are you the man that knocked me cold last night?"

He said, "Yes, Captain, I am."

---

*During the invasion of the Gilbert Islands, Rear Admiral Mullinnix served as Commander Task Group 52.3. He was embarked in the escort carrier USS Liscome Bay (CVE-56). Mullinnix was killed when his flagship was torpedoed and sunk on the morning of 23 November 1943.
**Captain John H. Cassady, USN, commanded the Saratoga from August 1943 to June 1944.
***Gunner's Mate First Class Harold L. Derry, USN.

He said, "Well, Chief Derry, that was a damn good right." So he made chief right there. In most of the stories like that about Bogan, he was a tough guy. That ship had a lot of characters.

We had a chaplain named Cook, the only chaplain on that ship.* He did both Protestant and Catholic services. Years later, when I lived in the San Francisco Bay area, I was telling somebody about him. I said I knew a Catholic chaplain had received a dispensation to attend the Presbyterian seminary in San Anselmo, California. This individual said, "Sure, that's Father Cook." He knew because he had lived in San Anselmo. That was such an unusual thing, especially when you realized the fact that that wasn't after Vatican II; that was before. But his viewpoint was that most Protestant services could be handled by a lay person, and if anybody objected to him, he'd gladly help somebody lead the service.

Services in port were held on the hangar deck. I remember going to the service, and Cook was a real naval officer. One time he going through his sermon, I guess, and there were some aviation metalsmiths banging on some metal parts down at the other end of the hangar deck. Chaplain Cook was going on in sonorous tones, and he said, "Pardon me." Then he walked down to where these men were working, and he just changed his entire character, from a

---
*Lieutenant Commander Ozias B. Cook, CHC, USN.

clergy person to a naval officer. When he got down to the other end, he was a naval officer, and he let those guys know what they should do, and where they should do it. By the time he got back, he was a clergy person again.

Q: Did you go to the Catholic service or Protestant?

Mr. Bond: I went to the Protestant services, and I must say I didn't go real regularly. As I said, having the chaplain's yeomen in our division sort of led the quartermasters to that. But he was very well liked on the ship. He just tried like hell to get us down to Australia, so the crew could have a little bit of a run there, but he was never able to swing that. That was too far away for the only carrier in the South Pacific to go.

Q: Did you have daily prayers from him over the 1MC?*

Mr. Bond: No.

Q: How would you characterize the relationship in general between the officers and enlisted men in that ship?

Mr. Bond: Well, I think it was pretty good, because on

---

*1MC was the official designation for the ship's general announcing system.

that ship there were an awful lot of people that had done a lot of duty in the Navy. The officers that were really running that ship were experienced officers, men that had spent three years as ensigns. They hadn't been really rapidly advanced, so they really knew their stuff. The junior officers traveled under that umbrella, and the men accepted the competency of the officers. There were also one hell of a lot of competent men on that ship. And the officers accepted the competency of the men.

Q: Would you say it was a sense of mutual respect?

Mr. Bond: Yes. I remember one officer, Joe Cannon. He was from Wisconsin too. He picked up the interesting nickname of "On Deck at the Water's Edge Cannon."

When we anchored, you see, because the flight deck and the anchor windlass room were enclosed, you couldn't see the anchoring gear from the bridge. So the first lieutenant was down in the anchor windlass room, and it really was a room. A phone circuit ran between there and the bridge, and they had a talker on each end. Well, for years it was any seaman with clean dungarees, but we were getting so many officers, we had to find things for them to do. So this young ensign, Joe Cannon, was put on the phone on the bridge.

When we were anchoring once, the captain ordered the

chain veered to 60 fathoms, or whatever. The first lieutenant wanted to know whether that meant the 60-fathom shackle would be on deck or at the water's edge. Now, on the <u>Saratoga</u>, that was a long ways between the hawsepipe and the water. So the talker down in the anchor windlass room said, "Is that on deck or at the water's edge?"

Cannon, who was on the bridge, turned and told the captain, "The anchor's on deck at the water's edge."

The captain said, "Somehow, I can't visualize that.

Another time, when Cannon was the junior officer of the deck in port, he was standing watch at the after gangway. There was a boat alongside in the morning, and he yelled down and said, "Coxswain, wipe those seats off." A lot of dew had condensed.

The coxswain said, "What's that?'

[Louder] "Wipe the seats off."

"What'd you say, sir."

[Still louder] "Wipe the seats off."

The boatswain's mate of the watch said, "Why don't you tell him to wipe the thwarts off?"

So Cannon said, "Wipe the thwarts off."

"Aye, aye, sir."

But, you know, these were sort of amusing things that went on.

Q: Well, where would the first lieutenant be in this

anchor windlass room? Did he have to look out through a hawsepipe to see, or what?

Mr. Bond: Well, down in the anchor windlass room, the anchor chains went down through the hawsepipes, and then you also had a bullnose there. Then they'd take the cover off the bullnose when the ship was anchoring, so he could get a pretty good view from the bullnose. But you had no view whatsoever from the bridge, especially when maneuvering the bow so you could moor to a buoy. Putting the hawsepipe in position where you could get those cables down to the buoy was really a tricky operation. The first lieutenant was basically conning the ship through this phone system. But this happened to be an anchoring situation.

But, by and large, there was much better respect between officers and enlisted on that ship than later, when I was on the little PCE(R).* On that ship very inexperienced junior officers were thrust into a lot of decision-making things. For many of the rated men on that crew, the minimum experience was two years of sea duty. They didn't have the respect of all the officers.

Q: I think you had a good story about Captain Ramsey, too,

---

*PCE(R) was the designation of a convoy escort (rescue) patrol craft in which Bond served later in World War II.

and Admiral Fletcher.*

Mr. Bond: That was when the Saratoga was torpedoed, and it was listing.** They hadn't got the sub, and there were cans running all around dropping depth charges, and the ship was listing more. Fletcher was up on the flag bridge, and he kept yelling down, "Duke, when are you going to counterflood? I think you ought to counterflood."

Ramsey kept saying, "Okay, Admiral, just wait a while."

Finally, Fletcher said, "Duke, when are you going to counterflood?"

Ramsey leaned back and looked up and said, "Goddammit, Admiral, I'm captain of this ship, and I'm not going to counterflood until I think it's right."

Fletcher said, "Yeah, I guess you are," and he went back. But Ramsey was such a quiet man that if he spoke up like that it would back Fletcher off. Fletcher really knew that he'd pushed him to the end right there. Ramsey was right, because he had the responsibility for his ship.

Q: The admiral on board during your time was Sherman, who

---

*Captain Dewitt C. "Duke" Ramsey, USN, commanded the Saratoga from May to October 1942. During the Guadalcanal invasion of August 1942, Vice Admiral Frank Jack Fletcher, USN, was embarked. He was Commander Task Force 61 and served as overall on-scene commander for the operation.
**On 31 August 1942 the Saratoga was torpedoed by the Japanese submarine I-26. No one was killed, but the ship was out of the war for three months until repaired.

also had a sense that he had to run things.*

Mr. Bond: Yes. I remember the first time I ever met Sherman. We had an outside ladder from the bridge down to the flight deck. It was about three decks. It had one little landing on the way, but it was a narrow ladder. One of the first times I was ever going up for watch on the bridge was when I was still standing supervised watches. I was within an inch of being late, and I was tearing up that ladder. This little guy was coming down, and we met at that little bit of landing. I was taller than he was, and when I saw over the bill of his cap, I saw two stars. Then I came to a halt and tried to get out of the way. I just about jumped off. Sherman said, "Son, how long have you been in the Navy?"

"About a year, sir."

He said, "Well, I've been in for almost 40 years, and people get out of my way now when I'm coming. When you're in 40 years, they'll get out of your way. Do you understand me?"

I said, "Yes, Admiral."

Q: You were talking earlier about the long times at sea, which meant a holdup on mail, food, and so forth. Does

---

*In July 1943, shortly after Bond reported to the Saratoga, Rear Admiral Frederick C. Sherman, USN, embarked in her as Commander Carrier Division One. He remained on board until shifting to the USS Bunker Hill (CV-17) for the invasion of the Marshall Islands in early 1944.

that mean that there was not underway replenishment for the ship at that phase of the war?

Mr. Bond: Not of mail. I never remember mail coming aboard at sea.

Q: Well, and probably not food either, from what you say.

Mr. Bond: No. Ammunition and oil were the things. For Christmas of '43 we were supposed to be at Funafuti, so the fleet post office sent our mail there. Instead, we went to San Francisco for a quick yard period and out.* After the yard period we went to Pearl, and we got our current mail there. After that we operated out in the Marshalls for a couple months, January and February, and then we were detached and sent south to Nouméa. We got to Nouméa and there was nothing there. The war had passed it by. Then we went on to Hobart, Tasmania, and fueled there. From there the Saratoga went around to the Indian Ocean and operated with the English fleet.

Our 1943 Christmas mail did not catch up with us until May 20, 1944. In that time, we had had just one little mail call of current mail in Pearl Harbor. We left a mail orderly in Pearl when we went out to the Marshalls, and he

---

*The ship underwent overhaul at San Francisco from 9 December 1943 to 3 January 1944.

was there sorting mail. One day they told him to gather up this mail—he had a couple hundred sacks—because he was going to join the ship. So he said, "Where am I going?"

They said, "Nouméa."

He said, "Oh, no, not Nouméa."

But he went to Nouméa anyway and no *Saratoga*. Then they took him to Brisbane. He said, "Now things are looking up." But there wasn't any *Saratoga* in Brisbane. Then they put him and his mail on a train down to Sydney. No *Saratoga* there. He was there a little while, and they told him to gather up his mail. He was going to the West Coast, so he went all the way across Australia by train. In western Australia they only run the trains in the daytime because drifting sand at night would derail them.

He spent the night at Coolgardie, West Australia, which was a rip-roaring mining town in the interior. As far as anybody knows, he was the only American sailor that ever got there. The pubs ran 24 hours a day because of the three shifts of the mines and all. He had quite an evening and never spent a penny. Then they packed him and his mail, and he went to Fremantle, the port for Perth, and the *Saratoga* wasn't there. He had to wait around for about a month. We came in on May 20, and he finally got to distribute his mail. He'd been separated from his ship almost since the first week in January.

Roger Bond #1 - 112

Q: He had some wonderful liberty along the way.

Mr. Bond: Yes, but he'd hardly been paid since he'd left Pearl Harbor. But people took care of him. One little detail was that the Australian railroads in those days changed rail gauge at each state line, and he had to transfer all that mail from one car to another. That mail service was really fouled up for a while by our moving irregularly.

Going back to the fall of 1943, after Efate we moved up to Espiritu Santo, and that was a big base. We operated out of there until late October.

Q: Was that more of a lull period?

Mr. Bond: Yes. This was all a lull period.

Now, at this time the crew of the Saratoga was trying to talk themselves into the fact that any day their relief was going to come, and we'd go back to the States. The guys that had been on board the ship since the beginning of the war had been more than a year and a half out of the States.*

We also had this theory that the ship couldn't do more than about 24 knots. It just so happened that in air

---
*The Saratoga had departed San Diego on 1 June 1942 for Pearl Harbor and was away from the continental United States until her arrival at San Francisco just over 18 months later.

operations that summer, we had never needed more speed.

Q: Because they had enough wind.

Mr. Bond: They had enough wind. And so the crew had all talked themselves into this. The Saratoga's engineers had done an extensive repair a few months before on one of the turbines, taken out all the stages (or blades), and welded them back in. It was really a major yard job, but the ship's crew had done that. This was supposed to support the "24-knot maximum" theory.

So we went out to support amphibious landings on Bougainville. They sent us up on the northeast side, and the Marines went into Empress Augusta Bay on the southwest shores of the island. The main Japanese air bases protecting Bougainville were an island of Buka and a place called Bonis. We hit those air bases on the 30th and 31st of October. That first morning, when I was on watch, we were going to hit the air bases, and the water was so calm that it was almost like it was oily. We knew we had to have over 30 knots of wind across the flight deck to launch aircraft, because we didn't have a catapult, which is another story.* So all of a sudden Captain Cassady came

---

*During operations an aircraft carrier steams directly into the wind in order to provide planes sufficient lift for takeoffs and landings. In still air, she creates a relative wind with the ship's speed.

in and quietly said, "Quartermaster, would you ring up 33 knots."

So I rang it up, and the atmosphere in that pilothouse was just electric. Everybody was watching that log dial. The captain, of course, had had all the boilers lit off, and that log just went up as we increased speed. At the time he gave the order, we were doing about 18, which was our usual standard speed.

Q: Are you talking about pit log?

Mr. Bond: Yes, the indicator up on the bulkhead. And it just went, you know, 18, 19, 20, 21, right up through. It hit 30 knots, and then it slowed down a little bit on 31, 32, 33. That ship was moving, I can tell you. You could just feel the vibration. Ever since the last torpedo, the starboard inboard propeller had had sort of a nick in it, and it made a clunk when you were at high speed. Boy, you could really tell because, see, at 30 knots, we were 315 RPM. But those big screws were moving at about nine RPMs to a knot after we got moving, so it was about 340 when we hit 33. Then we called the crew to general quarters. When that crew got on station, every guy on that ship knew that we were doing at least 30 knots, and a sinking feeling came over them. Obviously, all this big story--when the crew had convinced themselves the ship couldn't go faster than

24--was not valid.

Just before we went up there, the light carrier Princeton, CVL, came down and joined us.* We knew she wasn't a replacement for the Saratoga. We hit Buka and Bonis for two days and dropped everything on them that they had aboard ship to drop except torpedoes.

Of course, with all this high-speed running, we were fueling the destroyers just about every day, keeping them topped off. So then we went down south of Guadalcanal to rendezvous with tankers and also an ammunition ship and replenished ammunition and fuel. While the ship was there, a TBF torpedo plane flew out from shore, and, God, the word went around immediately that Halsey was aboard.** Halsey went, of course, to see the captain and Admiral Sherman right away.

Then they called the crew to the hangar deck, and they had the forward elevator raised up so it was like a stage. There was Halsey in a sort of sweat-stained shirt and shorts, and pith helmet. He looked like he needed a shave. Basically he said, "What we found out is that the Japanese have brought six heavy cruisers and two light cruisers down from Truk and they're in Rabaul. If those cruisers come

---
*The USS Princeton (CVL-23) was a light carrier, constructed on the hull of a light cruiser. At 32 knots, she had the speed of a fast carrier, but with a length of 622 feet and a standard displacement of 10,662 tons, she was considerably smaller and could carry fewer aircraft.
**Admiral William F. Halsey, Jr., USN, was Commander South Pacific Area and Force. As a captain Halsey had commanded the Saratoga from 1935 to 1937.

down on Empress Augusta Bay, all the Marines have protecting them there is four light cruisers." See, this was the whole tenor of that time down there--no big forces. You read about all these invasions, but our invasions were very small--small groups, small ships. We only had four light cruisers. They'd been under air attack, and two of them were damaged. And the beachhead was still pretty restricted, a couple hundred yards deep.

He said, "If those cruisers get down there, they'll plow that beachhead from one end to the other. You have got to stop them because nobody else can. I came out here to tell you this because I don't know what's going to happen. This is one of these few times when the very nature of the crisis means that people are going to be placed in imminent danger. I'm placing you there, and I'm not letting somebody else tell you. I came out to tell you myself. Where we're sending you, we haven't had any ships during this war. Rabaul is well fortified and well protected."

So we went up there, and the air group went in. We launched everything from both ships except one SBD that had engine trouble. They later got him flying and armed him with depth charges and he flew antisubmarine patrol. It was a squally day, so we ran into rain showers and hid. The air group went in with the fighters up and the torpedo planes and bombers pretty low. They came over the mountains, and I understand the Japanese radar was not as good as ours. They'd been bombed earlier by high-altitude B-17s, so they sent their interceptors up high.* We got the bombers in without any interference on the first strike. And every torpedo plane got a hit, every single one. Three of the torpedo planes flew their torpedoes into the ships. As I understand it, one pilot tried to drop it in several passes and he couldn't do it. He just plain flew it in. Dive bombers were very successful. The two light cruisers were still in a nest; the SBDs put the bombs right in between them, and the cruisers turned in on each other.

Commander Caldwell was the air group commander.** He carried no bomb in his torpedo plane, but he had a photographer. The photographer was killed, but he took super pictures and lots of them.*** They were all over the bulletin boards of the ship afterwards. The fighter group had shot down 97 Jap planes. Even the rear-seat men in a

---

*B-17s were land-based heavy bombers of the U.S. Army Air Forces.
**Commander Henry H. Caldwell, USN, was Commander Carrier Air Group 12. For an account of this 5 November 1943 raid on Rabaul, see Samuel Eliot Morison, Volume VI of United States Naval Operations in World War II (Boston: Little, Brown, 1950), pages 323-330. Morison reports that the Saratoga's strike group comprised 33 Hellcat fighter, 16 Avenger torpedo bombers, and 22 Dauntless dive-bombers.
***The man who took a number of pictures before being killed in Caldwell's plane was Photographer's Mate First Class Paul T. Barnett, USN. Although not identified with his byline, one of Barnett's pictures from the Rabaul raid appears in Volume VI of the Morison series.

couple of SBDs got kills.

When they came back, a lot of planes were damaged; they couldn't get their wheels down, or they were shot up. The pilots were given a choice: "Do you want to put it in the drink or just belly it in on the flight deck?" Most of the guys would rather put it on the flight deck than the drink. When Caldwell came in, his port wheel wouldn't come down, and he was waved off. As he flew by, he sort of shook his fist at the landing signal officer and made a tight turn into the circle. When he came in again, his tailhook would come down but not his left wheel. He just made a perfect landing on that ship and came to a stop and fell over. About six feet of the port wing was shot off, just all kinds of bullet holes. There were 87 shrapnel holes in the plane. His radioman, his photographer, and his gunner were all dead. He knew they'd been wounded, and that's why he didn't want to put it in the drink.

Q: In case they were still alive.

Mr. Bond: Right. Because he had no way of knowing whether they were alive or dead. He knew that he wasn't getting a response from them. That was a really sensational raid, and then we hightailed it.

Q: Had you and the rest of the crew had a sense of apprehension when you headed that way?

Mr. Bond: Oh, sure, and a lot of tension. They had a prayer meeting for the pilots, and it was really a very intense thing.

The Japs sent 60, 70 planes out but, strangely enough, not in a mass attack. They'd come in two at a time, one at a time. In that period of time Sherman's radio call sign was Jocko. He'd talk to our escorting ships and say, "This is Jocko. Jocko one, you take this one." Then the screen would let them have it. We always had the San Juan and San Diego on the quarters, two antiaircraft cruisers. They were Atlanta class; each one had 16 5-inch guns. And they just loved something like that. Every one of those Jap planes got shot down; each ship took a turn. Never would we have done anything like that. But I don't know, I guess single planes could get through the Japanese radar or escape detection enough to encourage them to think that they could do it with us. That was the first real air battle that we had when we used the F6F fighters.* They had been at Buka and Bonis, but there wasn't any air resistance there.

---

*The F6F Hellcat, built by Grumman, was the U.S. Navy's primary carrier fighter during the last two years of World War II. It had a top speed of 380 miles per hour and replaced the Grumman F4F (318 mph) that had been the workhorse earlier.

Q: When had they come aboard the Saratoga?

Mr. Bond: They'd come aboard maybe a month before. They'd flown on and off a couple of times before we went up to the operation.

Q: Where did you get them?

Mr. Bond: At Espiritu Santo. When the very first F6F took off from the ship, he went up and then dropped in the drink. We thought, "Oh, my God. Is this our new fighter?" But that was, I think, the last one that ever did that. The engine conked out. After that we just hightailed it out of the New Britain area, and Marine Air Group Two from Rendova was waiting to supply air coverage as soon as we got within range. Of course, this was all again high-speed steaming, and we got down and refueled again. And then, lo and behold, the Essex and another carrier showed up. We had heard about Essex-class carriers, but to actually see one that existed was really something.

It was on November 5 that we hit Rabaul, and then six days later the two carrier groups hit it again. These new ships went up on the north side, and we came up again on the south, and there really wasn't anything left to do. Everything had been taken care of in the first raid. Then

Roger Bond #1 - 121

we went back into Espiritu and got replacement planes. I think on the second raid we'd only flown 60-some aircraft off.

Q: I gather you were getting an increased knowledge and awareness of carrier operations as all these things went on.

Mr. Bond: Oh, yes, especially being up on the bridge and standing there listening to the captain discuss things with the air officer a couple of feet away from you. That was one thing about a cozy bridge. If the captain wanted privacy, he would have gone into his sea cabin, but Cassady was pretty open, anyway.

Q: What impressions did you form of him?

Mr. Bond: I'd have gone anywhere with John Cassady. I thought he was a super guy.

Q: Why do you say that? What specific qualities?

Mr. Bond: He was a top-notch seaman. He had a good sense of humor. He was a real Navy man. When we were out with the British, he was a top diplomat. He just brought all kinds of credit to the ship and the U.S. Navy there.

Q: I think a tribute to his diplomacy was the fact that he was later Commander Sixth Fleet.*

Mr. Bond: Yes, I think that might have something to do with it.

I remember while we were in Bremerton Navy Yard they made a lot of changes in the ship, especially up in officers' country. They cut down the size of the captain's cabin space. The shipyard people put in a new bulkhead and took out the one that the captain's clock was on. At this time I was working up in the quartermasters' storeroom, and Cassady wanted a replacement clock. Fritz Kirsch and I were up there, and we had two beautiful chrome clocks. So we had a nice mahogany base made in the carpenter's shop, mounted the clock on it, and took the whole thing up to the captain's cabin. One of these clocks just kept super time. Cassady said, "Is that a good clock, Bond?"

I said, "Yes, sir, this clock's as good as the ship's chronometer." About four hours later, the Marine orderly found me and said, "The captain wants to talk to you." The clock had already lost an hour.

When I got to the cabin, the first thing Cassady said was, "God help us if the ship's chronometers lose at this rate."

---
*As a vice admiral, Cassady served as Commander U.S. Sixth Fleet from 1952 to 1954.

I said, "Well, Captain, you got the wrong clock. There's two of them."

So, anyway, I got him the other one, which, of course, did keep good time. When he left the ship later, all the heads of departments were there. We had seven full commanders on that ship, and he said good-bye to them. He started off down the gangway, and he stopped, and came back. He said, "Now, remember, Bond, don't give Captain Moebus a clock like you gave me, because he hasn't got as good a sense of humor as I have."* And that was months after I'd made the change.

Speaking of Captain Moebus, he came aboard about 2:30 A.M., about two days before he was scheduled to arrive. The night quarterdeck watch had an officer of the deck, quartermaster, and a messenger. The quarterdeck was on the flight deck between the stack structure and the side of the ship; it then extended from the stack to the island structure. There was a light drizzle, and the quartermaster was in a little hatch, hunched over his desk and reading. The messenger and the OOD were sleeping in a shelter inside the stack structure.

Moebus appeared at the quartermaster's elbow without warning and asked to be logged in. The quartermaster, of course, was stunned. He was stammering some kind of

---

*Captain Lucian A. Moebus, USN, commanded the Saratoga from August 1944 to April 1945.

explanation about the OOD. His hat was on the back of his head, and his sidearm was hanging down like a cowboy's gun belt because he had relieved a man of goodly girth and hadn't bothered to adjust the belt. Moebus calmed him down, told him to let the officer of the deck and the messenger sleep. All the quartermaster had to do was tell him where his cabin was. The captain handled his own bag. It turned out that the bunk was made up, and there was no further contact.

Can you imagine the reaction of the OOD when he went to fill out the supposedly dull, routine midwatch log? He had lost his opportunity to be the first to greet his new captain.

Q: Your story on Captain Cassady suggests that he had a good memory for detail.

Mr. Bond: Yes. The crew wasn't a faceless mob with him. When he had the chance, he always saw to it that the crew got ashore or got something. Another thing I really liked about him was his seamanship.

Q: What examples do you have of that?

Mr. Bond: He took over command at Efate; that was a very tight harbor. He really had to deal without much personal experience of the characteristics of the ship when he took it out the first time. And the Saratoga was a hard ship to handle. You had to put some speed past that rudder to get any action. You had to be a long ways ahead of time; her turning circle at 15 knots was about 2,000 yards.

Q: She had a lot of sail area too.*

Mr. Bond: That's right. That's right.

Then we went over to India and Trincomalee, Ceylon, where we moored bow and stern to buoys. So to take a ship of that size and just bring her in and set her down between those two buoys and toss a line over was pretty good work. All the British ships there were watching, and they really appreciated that kind of ship handling. I've seen destroyer captains that handle their ships about like motor launches when they bring them alongside. That's one thing, but doing it with a carrier, why, that's something else.

Q: In what ways did the British express their appreciation?

Mr. Bond: Well, they were very good on sending messages, and some were light-hearted, like that one I told you about

---

*Sail area is a ship's vertical hull surface on which the wind exerts force. In the case of the Saratoga her prominent smokestack arrangement also served as a sail.

the *Victorious*: "We fried them, and baked them, and broiled them. Now how the hell do you cook them?"

One time when we were at sea refueling the destroyers, we fueled our three before the *Illustrious* fueled her two. The rear admiral of the British aircraft carriers sent a message over to Cassady and said, "John, if I were the calf, I'd rather you were the cow than Bill." Other times, they'd send over something like, "Nice bit of work," or something of that sort. They did that very openly, much more than the American Navy would do.

The British have a reputation for being reserved, but we were really more reserved than the British were. They might be reserved in a formal social gathering or something, but in a professional way they expressed themselves much more, in a very friendly way.

Q: On the subject of ship handling, as a quartermaster, you must have steered the *Saratoga*.

Mr. Bond: Oh, sure.

Q: What was that like?

Mr. Bond: Well, in the first place, it didn't have a wheel. It had a little controller, like a trolley car. Most of the time at sea, we kept pretty good speed on it.

Of course, the ship was always zigzagging, especially when one of the quartermasters was on the wheel, because you'd be at general quarters or special sea detail.* Those were two of the times that we steered. You had to kick the rudder hard to get the ship moving and also to stop it moving. And you had to anticipate it because you could swing past the right course very easily. There was a lot of momentum. But it was particularly tricky in slow speeds, and that's when you were entering or leaving port. And particularly Pearl Harbor, which is pretty tight, so they don't want you to go very fast in there. So you come in Pearl at five knots or something like that.

Q: That doesn't give you much action on the rudder.

Mr. Bond: No, you really have to look ahead.

The Saratoga almost always tied up to mooring quays on Ford Island, unless you were in the shipyard. Normally we went in at Berth Fox Two or Three, which are on the submarine base side. So we'd go down on the west side of Ford Island. Then, as you came around, you'd need a tug because with that sail and that slow a speed, you just couldn't make the turn in the channel.

---

*Zigzagging is the practice of steering a series of relatively short straight-line variations from the intended base course. The purpose is to make it more difficult for a submarine to plot a target ship's course as part of the torpedo-firing solution.

One time we were coming in and Cassady said, "Come right ten degrees rudder."

With a questioning tone I said, "Come right, ten degrees rudder?"

He said, "Yes, come right."

Well, this time we went down the east side of the island, and a tug took us all the way around. We came back, and we tied up. The sea detail hadn't been secured yet, but we were alongside, and I was just sort of standing there by the helm. Cassady said, "I'm really glad you questioned me about that because that shows you're involved. That damn garbage scow was coming down the west channel, and I just didn't want to get in any problem with him, so that's why I came down here. But I really appreciate the fact that the quartermaster is thinking with me, and is thinking ahead, and anticipating. That's a comfort because it's perfectly possible for me to mean left and say right. Everybody can do that."

Q: He just didn't want you just blindly following orders.

Mr. Bond: Right, and I appreciated that very much too.

Q: That's another nice personal touch.

Mr. Bond: Right, and, you know, it wasn't only me. He treated everybody that way.

He seemed to go on the basis that everybody had a job, and he respected you and your job. Whatever rank or rate went along with it was immaterial. I mean, he was looking to you as his quartermaster, or he was looking to you as his officer of the deck, or gunnery officer, whatever capacity it was.

Q: I can imagine that some skippers would chew out a helmsman for questioning an order.

Mr. Bond: Yes, but not of that rank. A lot of them wouldn't have said anything. Later I was on that little PCE(R), which had all kinds of maneuverability. We could put one engine ahead, one engine astern, and we could turn right on the spot, the screws were so far out. And I remember one time tying up in East Loch in Pearl, and we were supposed to tie to a buoy, and the captain couldn't keep it close enough to the buoy. We kept paying out line, paying out line and finally we were three ship lengths from the buoy. That was really embarrassing. You looked around at those other ships, and you wondered if you had any friends on these ships that knew you were there.

Q: Did you steer the <u>Saufley</u> at all?

Mr. Bond: No, I never did.

Q: So you don't have a basis for comparison, really.

Mr. Bond: No. I, of course, steered the PCE(R) a lot.

Cassady was a very human person and very straightforward, no bombast to him. He wasn't as gentle as Mullinnix. He wasn't as bombastic as Bogan. He was his own man, but he had a lot of personality. He definitely commanded the ship and was in command of the situation. Sherman respected him a lot. That was another thing that you got right away, that Sherman really liked Cassady.

Q: How did you know that?

Mr. Bond: Just by the way he treated Cassady. He'd ask Cassady's advice, and we could see the kidding that went back and forth. And Sherman passed a number of compliments to him. But when we went out to India, there was no flag; Cassady was the senior officer present afloat of the task group, the three destroyers and ourselves.

In late November we went up in the Gilberts, and we saw the Liscome Bay blow up, but we didn't know it was Liscome Bay at that time.* We found out shortly after.

---

*The escort carrier Liscome Bay (CVE-56) was torpedoed and sunk by the Japanese submarine I-175 on the morning of 24 November 1943 while supporting the invasion of the Gilbert Islands. Of those on board, 624 were lost and 272 were rescued. Among those killed was Rear Admiral Henry M. Mullinnix, USN, embarked as Commander Task Group 52.3.

Of course, we knew that Mullinnix was on it, and that was quite a shock. But the damndest thing in the Gilberts was that one day we saw 13 carriers. Here a month before that, we wondered where all the people in the world were. We were hoping for a replacement and thinking in terms of the Ranger or the Enterprise as the only two carriers left in the world. That was some day, I'll tell you.

One interesting thing we had there--one night we were moving along and picked up an unidentified ship. It was a pretty good-size ship moving along at pretty good speed. Sherman was talking to the commander of the screen and decided to launch a torpedo attack. They saw no IFF signal or anything else while they were talking about this ship and the course and speed.* They were using their call signs, "Jocko One" and "Jocko Three," back and forth. Finally Jocko gave the word, "When you get the correct radar setup, open fire."

All of a sudden a voice broke in, "Jocko, Jocko, don't open fire. We are a friendly ship traveling on the course and speed that you're tracking. Don't open fire, don't open fire." It was the heavy cruiser Baltimore. It was her first cruise out there.

---

*IFF--identification, friend or foe--is an electronic signal that shows up on the radar screen of the unit that detects a ship or aircraft. It enables the radar operator to determine whether the target on his screen is friendly.

Bond #1 - 132

Q: They finally figured out who the admiral was discussing.

Mr. Bond: Yes, and you can imagine these <u>Baltimore</u> guys listening on the radio and then saying, "That's us they're talking about."

About this time the <u>Princeton</u>'s steering gear was breaking down all the time. We'd be zigzagging, and they'd go off on the far horizon. They kept saying, "Request permission to be detached."

Sherman sent back, "Don't be silly. You're good for another year out here."

But it was getting bad, so they finally were detached and went towards Pearl. And that's the last we saw of them until we were leaving San Francisco in January 1944 and passed them coming in.

Q: Do you have any other memories of the Gilberts operation?

Mr. Bond: No. We flew a lot of sorties. We didn't get into the islands at all. We never anchored or anything else. The biggest memory of the Gilberts operation was all those damn ships. We looked in the signal book and saw all these ships that we didn't know existed. That was a profound experience.

Q: After the Gilberts came your yard period in San Francisco.

Mr. Bond: Captain Cassady really was given credit for getting us back to Hunters Point in '43.* We had a condenser problem, and the Pearl Harbor Navy Yard could have fixed it just as easy. He talked somebody into letting us go back to Hunters Point. So we went back and we were there only about three and a half weeks, but everybody got eight days' leave.

Of course, the Saratoga had piled up enormous amounts of money in the ship's service fund. I happened to be on the leave party that was fortunate enough to be home for Christmas. During that time they had a Christmas party at the Palace Hotel for the crew. It was two nights, so that half went one night and half went the other. Of course, it was really a fourth each night, because half were gone. But I remember there were two orchestras. I forget who the second one was, but they flew up Kay Kyser and his band.** The ship chartered a plane and flew them up. And I guess it was just some kind of a party. The captain figured, "What the hell? The ship's accumulating all this money out

---

*Hunters Point was the location of the San Francisco shipyard where the Saratoga was repaired in December 1943 and January 1944.
**Kay Kyser was a popular big-band leader of the era; he also appeared in a number of comedy movies.

where there's no place to spend it." For instance, every time somebody bought a carton of cigarettes, two cents went into the thing, and then mark-up on all the ship's service stuff. But things like that indicated that he was a pretty savvy individual.

Q: What did your leave consist of?

Mr. Bond: Well, it was an eight-day leave, and I went down to Los Angeles. I took Fritz Kirsch with me because he's from Chicago and couldn't go home. I think we did have a limitation of not being able to go very far.

Q: Did you take up with your future wife again at that point?

Mr. Bond: Yes. There was one interesting deal. At the time I still had someone else that I really considered my girlfriend, but I asked Marilyn out. We were going to go to the Coconut Grove. I think it was Wednesday. Then I asked Ann out for another night, say Thursday. But she couldn't go Thursday. So then I called Marilyn, my future wife, and said, "Oh, my mother has some friends in town and they're planning something Wednesday night. Could you go out Thursday night instead?"

Marilyn said, "Sure."

So I took Ann to the Coconut Grove Wednesday night. Now, Marilyn is very nearsighted. Without her glasses, she can hardly see the floor. It was always a joke. She'd go to the ladies' room and say, "Wait here." You'd move ten steps away and watch her come out and try and find you. And vain, you know, she didn't want to wear her glasses. So she wasn't wearing her glasses Wednesday night, but I got a tap on her shoulder and this, "Hi." It was Marilyn, who was there too. Just after I called and broke our date, this guy who happened to be Milo Bekins of Bekins Van Lines called her and wanted to know if she wanted to go out. She said, "Sure."

Q: And you had some fast explaining to do.

Mr. Bond: Well, she just thought it was funny and still does to this day. Then she and I went there the next night. And she didn't care. She'd go hear Freddie Martin ten nights in a row.

But that incident made a very good impression on me, the fact that she had such a good sense of humor because, I tell you, I could have dug a hole in the dance floor.

Q: I'm sure.

Mr. Bond: That was a pretty good little leave. Then,

after we got our condenser fixed, the ship took off again. First of all, right after we got out of Hunters Point, we went out and anchored at the port of embarkation. There we brought aboard a group of Seabees that we were going to take out to Pearl.* You would have thought they were going to make a landing in the Farallons or something.** It was sort of drizzly, and they were in camouflaged ponchos with helmets and all. The ship was putting the Seabees all over the place. They put about 50 of them up in the anchor windlass room; they rigged cots up there.

Then I went to special sea detail. We started out and, of course, off the Pacific Coast you run into a large swell. The Saratoga's pitching axis was far aft. It was aft of the center of the ship, and that meant that your bow was rising and falling probably like ten stories or something between the bottom and the top. When I came down from that special sea detail, it was as close as I ever came to being seasick in my life. These poor guys that were rough and tough when they were coming aboard were now rolling on the deck. Almost all of them were trying to get into that small head up there. The ones that weren't were the few that were trying to get out. I took one look at that and smelled all that, and I just turned and left. But, boy, those poor guys were really reduced in the space

---
*Seabees is the nickname for members of the Navy's mobile construction battalions (CB's).
**The Farallon Islands are about 30 miles west of San Francisco's Golden Gate.

of an hour.

Q: And they weren't used to riding the ship.

Mr. Bond: No, no. But, anyway, we went and got out to Pearl. We were there just about a week or so, and then we went out to the invasion of the Marshalls. The first attacks were at Kwajalein and Wotje. The Navy tried to avoid the problems at Tarawa, where they hadn't done enough preliminary bombardment. We really did it this time. They just bombarded the beach every night, about five or six nights. When the last salvo went each morning, the first planes came in, and we had a lot of carriers there. That was pretty quick. We went in the lagoon there, but I didn't go ashore. There wasn't very much to see.

Then we went up to Eniwetok Atoll, and we took care of it. We had the Princeton back with us by this time; it caught up. That deal was a ten-day preparation. And when we went in there in that lagoon, a TBM landed, and it was, believe me, the biggest thing on those islands.* It was the only thing that was over knee-high. Those islands were secured in 365 minutes. It took that long for some of the Japs to dig out. And talk about the Japanese not surrendering, they surrendered there. The guys said they

---

*TBM was the designation for the General Motors version of the Grumman TBF Avenger torpedo-bomber.

were literally punch-drunk. Well, a friend of mine was coxswain of a whaleboat. Those were the only boats we carried with us, two whaleboats. Cassady had to go ashore, so I went along as bowhook in the boat crew. So he and I wandered around a little bit, and, boy, that island was just completely plowed by gunfire and bombs.

Then it was from there that we were sent down south, and we were going into Hobart because we had to fuel. I think they picked Hobart because it was sort of out of the way, which reduced the publicity. We ran into a storm that came right out of the Antarctic. It was one of the worst storms that the weather bureau had had. Those swells in that southern ocean were so long that we were taking every one over the bow, and the cans were just downhill and uphill and downhill and uphill. They really enjoyed watching us pound. At that time the Saratoga had some 20-millimeter guns in sponsons up towards the bow. Those were carried away in that storm, along with a lot of the planking off the bow of the flight deck.

Then we came into Hobart. The coast was rocky, and it was gray and stormy, and we started up the Derwent River. We'd come around the bend and it'd be a little bit softer, and the clouds were breaking up, and you'd see farms. You'd come around another bend, it'd be a little better, and the skies were lightening up. Then we came around another bend and found that Hobart was built at the bend of the river, just like an amphitheater. Then the sun came out. We tied up there, and they declared a school holiday. We were the first aircraft carrier that had ever been in there, and the first American Navy ship. I was on watch till noon, and liberty ran from noon to midnight. After I was relieved of watch, which was pretty quick, I went down, changed into my dress blues, and had a bite to eat. By the time I got up topside again, they were already bringing the drunks aboard. [Laughter]

We went down the end of the pier, across the street and there was a pub. Over the door it said "Cascade Beer." I swear, half the crew--that's all they saw of Hobart because they were carried out.

This fellow Les Shryer and I were together, and we went in there and had a couple of beers. Aussie beer is strong, and it was seven pence a glass. Their pound was $3.26 so that made it about eight cents. Then they sold whiskey by the glass, and it was darn near a water glass for a shilling, 16 cents. Of course, these guys had been at sea so long they believed their own lies about how much they could drink.

We went on uptown, looking around, and we went into an ice cream parlor for a snack. We got talking to a fellow there, and he was off that day and he said he'd just love to take us around. He had a 1939 Plymouth, and he drove us around. There was a mountain. We went way up Mount

Wellington and looked over everything. Afterwards we found out that the Australian gas ration was four gallons a month if you didn't have any defense needs. With his 1939 Plymouth, I think he blew a month's worth of gas on us.

He worked at a fruit cannery. At the end of the tour he took us there for a taste of apples and pears. When he saw how much we enjoyed the fresh fruit, he said he would return us to the ship at midnight. We said, "No, you don't have to do any more." That didn't seem to do any good, because there he was with a full crate of pears and apples. He would not allow us to pay for them. He told us his boss had insisted that we take a full crate each. Even though it was midnight, there were enough people awake to eat the whole contents that night. You have no idea how good fresh fruit tastes after a long period at sea.

Roger Bond #2 - 141

Interview Number 2 with Mr. Roger Bond

Place: The home of Mr. Bond's daughter, Charlene Peterson, Oakdale, Minnesota

Date: Saturday, 17 October 1987

Interviewer: Paul Stillwell

Q: One of the interesting facets of life in the prewar Navy was that a few men stayed in the same ship for years and years. You discovered when you were on board the Saratoga in the 1940s that two of the original plank owners from the late '20s were still there. What do you recall of them?

Mr. Bond: One was a machinist's mate by the name of Johnson, and the other was a chief electrician's mate by the name of Pop Blanchard.* Johnson was a pretty quiet man, and I never really knew very much about his personality. He was somewhat aloof, and he was an introspective, technician-type of individual. But Blanchard was very gregarious, probably the best-known man on the ship.

Blanchard had 25 or 26 years in the Navy, and he didn't make chief until after he'd been in about 22 years.

---
*Chief Machinist's Mate Oscar Johnson, USN; Chief Electrician's Mate Frederic L. Blanchard, USN.

I remember we got a Look magazine or something with a big picture of Victor Mature, who'd joined the Coast Guard as apprentice seaman and in a little less than three years had made chief boatswain's mate.* That was nothing against Blanchard, because the system had changed. In our way of thinking, if you made coxswain, you must have received favoritism.** For Victor Mature to make chief boatswain's mate in three years was not seen as admirable. But someone put Mature's picture up by Blanchard's bunk and wrote on it, "He came up the hard way, too, Pop."

Q: Did these two men talk about their years on board the Saratoga?

Mr. Bond: Well, Blanchard would, and now he's dead. And, as I say, I never really got to know Johnson at all or have any real conversation with him that I can remember. He was a very quiet person. Blanchard would talk about all the really famous people that'd been on the ship, and places they'd gone. For instance, those two guys were on the Saratoga the first time it went through the Panama Canal. The ship was so wide on the flight deck that it took down all the lampposts on the sides of the locks. The next time the canal authority took them down before the ship did. We

---
*Victor Mature was a handsome movie actor of the era.
**At that time the rate of coxswain, a petty officer third class, was the equivalent of the present rate of boatswain's mate third class.

heard stories like that.

I think that both of those guys were in the yards, too, and assigned to the ship quite a while before the commissioning; they were in the nucleus crew.* They talked about the thrill of it, because at that time the "Lex" and the "Sara" were the first genuine aircraft carriers, and it was an exciting thing. Blanchard said the Navy was really looking forward to having these ships, and they knew that they were on the verge of opening up all new avenues. So that was the main thing I remember about Blanchard. He was just a very easy man to know, very friendly to everybody.

Q: Did Blanchard specifically talk about why they never transferred?

Mr. Bond: They just didn't see any reason to move out of the neighborhood they enjoyed. I think they really realized that they were in a special category, and they weren't going to give that up. If the ship had stayed in commission, I think both of them would have probably been there until they retired, just to make it a complete thing. When you're one of hundreds of plank owners, being a plank

---

*Saratoga was built by the New York Shipbuilding Company, Camden, New Jersey, and commissioned on 16 November 1927. During World War II the ship's muster rolls still showed both men as having reported aboard 11-16-27.

owner isn't anything special. I mean, the day of commissioning everybody is. But as the years pass, it becomes more of a select group. When you get down to the last few, they want to preserve that. Those two had no interest whatsoever in getting off the ship.

Q: Do you know if they stayed around until she was decommissioned?

Mr. Bond: That I'm not sure of at all. I would guess so. I would be amazed if they weren't. From what I feel of the Navy in those days, no one would have ordered them off the ship. It was just one of those exceptional things. You might have wanted a chief electrician's mate in the worst way, but you weren't going to requisition one from the Saratoga.

Q: It's a point worth making that this is something that only an enlisted man can do. An officer couldn't have had his career pattern for that long in one ship.

Mr. Bond: No, I wouldn't think so. Although our chief quartermaster Gain told me that there were a number of merchant officers that came in the Navy in World War I, and a few of them stayed in. They did, of course, revert to a lower rank, and most of those men that he knew of were assigned to duties like tankers, and they were stuck there a long time. They were out of the mainstream of advancement, and there was no sense in those fellows having experience in different assignments.

Q: And a tanker was essentially a merchant-type ship.

Mr. Bond: That's right. And then there were several others that were on Navy supply ships, AKs or something.

Q: During our discussion last night, you were on the verge of the Indian Ocean venture. Could you resume, please.

Mr. Bond: Well, I think I was mentioning that we had met this fellow who worked for a fruit-processing company. He took us by his plant, and they gave us a crate of apples and pears, and Tasman apples are wonderful apples. They're like Jonathans, and they were very well appreciated back on the ship. We even managed to get a couple of them out of the crate while our shipmates ate the rest.

We proceeded from Hobart to Fremantle in West Australia. At Fremantle several Australian radiomen--as I recall, they were called telegraphers--and a leading signalman, a fellow by the name of Larry Ennis, joined the *Saratoga*. With Larry came three sets of signal flags, as used by the Royal Navy. This was really an awesome array of signal flags because they didn't use flags for two purposes like we did. They had all the international alphabet flags, and they had their own set of alphabet flags. Then they had all sorts of special-purpose flags for signals where we would use one of the alphabet flags by itself.

We were to join the British Far Eastern Fleet, using Royal Navy procedures. We also had the Royal Navy signal book, so we made up some sheets depicting the flags and what they were. They were mounted on the stand with our long glasses. Larry Ennis was pretty much required to be on the signal bridge from daylight to dusk. After a couple of weeks, we became pretty proficient in British procedures, too, because our signalmen were capable, intelligent fellows.

Then when we rendezvoused with the fleet and proceeded to Trincomalee, which is a naval base in Ceylon, the country now known as Sri Lanka. Trincomalee was a large harbor with a very small town. They had several floating dry docks and navy installations there. It was somewhat like Pearl Harbor in that it had several bays or arms in the harbor but a much larger open entrance than at Pearl. The bays were sort of restricted and tight, and the major ships tied to buoys fore and aft.

The British fleet there was built around the battle cruiser _Renown_ and the battleships _Queen Elizabeth_ and

Valiant. Those three ships all participated in World War I. Then there was the aircraft carrier Illustrious, which was a sister ship to the Victorious, which had operated with us just about a year before. Then there were a number of heavy and light cruisers. The only ones I can remember are the heavy cruisers London and Sussex.

The French battleship Richelieu was also part of the fleet. She was a very advanced, modern battleship, but the French were not too friendly. The hospitality on the Richelieu was almost nonexistent and limited to formal invitations. They were very jealous of some of the French technical innovations. For one thing, their main battery guns could be reloaded while elevated, whereas ours and those in other navies had to be brought down to zero elevation for reloading. No American was going to be allowed anywhere near those turrets, which we thought was rather odd since the ship was full of American antiaircraft guns and radar that we'd put aboard.*

We also had in the fleet the Dutch light cruiser Tromp and two Dutch destroyers, the Van Galen and Tjerk Hiddes.** They were good little ships. The Tromp was

---
*The Richelieu was almost finished when France surrendered to Germany in June 1940. The ship escaped to Senegal and was subsequently completed at the New York Navy Yard in 1943. That year she served with the British Home Fleet and in 1944-45 with the British Pacific Fleet.
**The Van Galen (ex-Noble) and Tjerk Hiddes (ex-Nonpareil) were former British destroyers that the Royal Navy transferred to the Royal Netherlands Navy in 1942.

really a small light cruiser.* There were a couple of Australian destroyers in the fleet too; HMAS Napier was one. All in all, there were about 55 ships.** We'd brought with us the American destroyers Dunlap, Fanning, and Cummings. The Cummings was 365, the Dunlap was 384, and the Fanning was 385.

Q: I marvel at your ability to recall all these names.

Mr. Bond: Well, you know, it's like recalling an old neighborhood. I mean, you know that hill there outside your house. Well, my "house" we had ships outside.

Those three were in what was really that first post-World War I class of destroyers, after the flush-deck four-stackers.***

Q: One other thing that you mentioned the other day on these signal flags was that your hoists weren't long enough to accommodate all those signals.

---

*The Tromp, built in the Netherlands and completed in 1938, had a standard displacement of 3,787 tons and mounted six 6-inch guns. By comparison, the U.S. Cleveland (CL-55)-class light cruisers had a standard displacement of 11,744 tons and carried 12 6-inch guns apiece.
**For more detail on these operations, see Clark G. Reynolds, "'Sara' in the East," U.S. Naval Institute Proceedings, December 1961, pages 74-83.
***The last of the four-stackers, the USS Pruitt (DD-347), was commissioned in September 1920. The new broken-deck "gold-platers" began going into commission with the Farragut (DD-348) in June 1934. The Cummings was commissioned in 1936 and the Dunlap and Fanning in 1937.

Mr. Bond: Oh, yes. The British could make up a flag hoist of 13 flags, as I recall. In the American Navy the most flags you'd ever get in the hoist was eight. And the only way you got into eight was when you had a four-digit time. Half the time we'd put that signal on two hoists anyway, but that was the maximum. So our yardarms were spaced to allow about eight flags. Here the guys would still be calling out flags when the hoist was two-blocked and you had them all on the deck around your feet.* So we had a catwalk that ran from the signal bridge back to the stack structure. One guy would go tearing along the catwalk with the end of the hoist and string it out like laundry.

It took three flags for the British to report a man overboard--fox, fishery, church pennant, I think. The U.S. Navy signal for that was the five flag at the dip. The British had all these flags, and they even used the church pennant. Another thing, they had were two affirmative flags, and it depended on whether you were replying to a senior or a junior. One was, I guess, "Yes," and the other one was, "Yes, sir." Anyway, we didn't have any problem with that because we were junior to everybody, being the foreigner.

---

*Two-blocked was when a hoist (or tackle) was all the way up to the block on the yardarm and the flag (or tackle block) was up against it. Having the two blocks together produced the term.

Q: Did you wind up having a fair amount of dealing with the signalmen?

Mr. Bond: Well, I did because I always wanted to improve my proficiency in signaling. I wanted to be ready for when I got back in destroyers, because in the smaller ships signalmen and quartermasters were mixed and handled duties jointly.

When we moored at Trincomalee, the battleship *Valiant* was immediately astern of us. Her bow was tied on the same buoy as our stern. I became acquainted, by semaphore, with a signalman on the *Valiant*, and he invited me to go over to the Royal Navy canteen with him. The *Valiant*'s boat stopped by the *Saratoga*, and I hopped aboard. He was a kid from just out of London, Croydon, and we became pretty good friends. I have to admit that we circumvented American Navy censors by the fact that I gave Lenny the address for Marilyn, who is my present wife, and he wrote to her. In the British Navy they could say where they were and what they were doing. In fact, their mail was postmarked through the Ceylonese postal system and had stamps from Ceylon on it. So when he introduced himself and said I had given him her name, she, of course, knew where we were.

I remember we were going over to the Royal Navy canteen, and Lenny was apologizing for the fact that they had reduced the beer allotment. They'd give you a chit to buy a bottle of beer, and then, of course, you paid for it too. They had just cut it down from six bottles to four bottles, but in the American Navy the custom was really two cans of beer. I thought, "Well, that's still pretty generous." And then the British beer is a little stronger too. When we got there, I found out they were really quart bottles. I just had trouble believing that these guys could drink six quarts of warm beer 8 degrees latitude from the equator. But they did. So that was really an interesting place to go with all these nationalities that were there.

There was also an Italian sloop-of-war that was there; she had defected from the Japanese after Italy fell. She wasn't really operating, but her sailors were around there. I think she did a little antisubmarine work. So we had quite a United Nations assembly then.

Q: I'd be interested in hearing how the Saratoga moored her stern to a buoy. I hadn't heard of that previously.

Mr. Bond: Well, we did it basically with cables and wire. We had a windlass astern; and we had a hawse there. Captain Cassady would bring it in and nose the bow in to a buoy ahead. Most of the time the prevailing wind was such that after we moored the bow, the wind would push against our sail and move us right in to the buoy astern. Now, these were large buoys; you could put about seven or eight men on one of them. So as soon as one of our boatswain's mates got where he could heave a line on it--and you could heave a line a long ways from the height of our flight deck--and then they'd bring the cables out and shackle them into the buoy. It really was not a big operation.

I do recall that one day when we had a wind off the land, we did have a tug assist because of that large sail. The British radarmen said that because of her large stack they could pick up the Saratoga farther away than they ever picked up a target before.

Q: That's understandable. Of course, she was built long before radar was commonplace.

Mr. Bond: The routine there seemed to be to go out on Monday and get back in Friday. Then you could have an inspection on Saturday, and then have a regatta on Sunday. Of course, as you might expect, when we got there the captain wanted to make sure we looked pretty good and the ship looked pretty good. So the first weekend he held regular captain's inspection.

Then the British rear admiral on the aircraft carriers inspected us the next Saturday.* He was in white shorts

---

*This was Rear Admiral Clement Moody, RN, who had his flag in the Illustrious. He had tactical command of the two carriers, Illustrious and Saratoga, in Task Force 70.

and an open-neck white shirt. We were all in undress whites and jumpers. He took his time and looked each one of us over. And then the next week the vice admiral of the battle fleet inspected us, and he, also, was in shorts and open-neck shirt and looked us all over, one by one.* And then, believe it or not, the admiral of all admirals, Admiral Somerville, Commander in Chief of the British Far Eastern Fleet, inspected us the next week.** And he was in shorts and an open-neck shirt.

Q: That could take a while, to inspect so many men.

Mr. Bond: Yes, about that time the crew was probably 2,200 to 2,400 men. So we really thought we had worked through the roster by then. Then we found out that Lord Louie Mountbatten, whose headquarters for the whole China-Burma-India theater were in Kandy, Ceylon, was coming down to look us over.*** When he arrived, I happened to be quartermaster of the watch, and the first thing that struck us was he was <u>not</u> in shorts and an open-neck shirt. Of course, the British Navy does have a uniform similar to the American naval whites, with the choke collar, and that's what he wore. The quarterdeck on the Saratoga was located in that space on the flight deck between the bridge

---
*Vice Admiral Sir Arthur Power, RN.
**Admiral Sir James F. Somerville, RN.
***Admiral Lord Louis Mountbatten, RN, Supreme Allied Commander, Southeast Asia.

structure and the stack structure. He went out and he looked towards the bow, he looked towards the stern, and he said, "They look very good. Now let's bring them all together in the shade of the stack."

Q: That was his inspection.

Mr. Bond: That was his inspection. He just took it in one panoramic view. Then we brought all the crew, still in formation, into a mass. He got up on a little podium they made there, and he said, "Can you hear me?" Of course, when you say that to a couple thousand sailors, somebody's going to say, "No."

So he said, "Well, just break ranks, come on in." And they crowded in. Then he started telling them about the war in the China-Burma-India theater; why the Saratoga had been requested; why the war seemed to go slowly; and why there was no blitzkrieg type of operation. I think that was pretty edifying for most everybody, because we really didn't know about it. He said that this Italian sloop-of-war had defected from Singapore and brought the information that there were three Jap carriers and five battleships in Singapore. We were essentially trying to lure them out.

Q: And if not that, you had them neutralized.

Mr. Bond: Yes, that's true. That's true. Because with our force, they couldn't leave the area unprotected.

Q: How did the crew respond to Mountbatten's visit?

Mr. Bond: They really thought he was the greatest thing they'd ever seen--from the British Navy anyway. He said, "I just wish I could go with you." He said, "I know what you're thinking, but I really do wish. I remember back when we were on destroyers in the war in 1939 and '40. We'd been tossed around that English Channel. We'd come in and get a little bit of fuel and food, and some gray-haired old bastard from Whitehall would come down and say, 'Go to it, lads. I wish I were with you.' We'd grit our teeth and say, 'Yeah, you'll be in bed with your old lady when we're out.' But I really would like to go."*

But our crew really identified with that kind of talk coming from that kind of man, and they thought he was something. I might say the British sailors thought he was something too. Because they considered him a sailor primarily. He'd proved himself to be a ship's officer. Whatever he was doing now, that was all right because he had shown them what he really could do.

I think the next week they began rotating a few ships

*Whitehall was the site of the headquarters of the Admiralty in London.

over to Colombo, a fairly large city on the other side of Ceylon. I had the feeling then that there were over 500,000 people but less than a million. That was a place where you really had a chance to go on liberty. There was nothing in that little village of Trincomalee. The main thing we did in Trincomalee was either go to the Navy canteen or watch sporting events. The British services tried to keep up a lot of athletics in areas like that, but in Colombo you could really go in the city.

Q: Well, there's some marvelous scenery in Ceylon too. Did you get out and see that?

Mr. Bond: Oh, just a little bit. We took some tours out from Colombo, and the ship arranged for some of that. But I didn't get up to Kandy and the mountains where I'd really like to have gone.

But one thing I might mention, growing up in the United States, in our history books and all, we read about the English stabilizing India. I guess they "conquered," but they stopped all the warfare that was going on, they brought peace, built roads, trained the civil service, and all that. But nothing prepared us for the experience of being hated in Ceylon. We didn't realize that the Indians hated the English. There were so many uniforms around, and most of the Ceylonese didn't really appreciate the difference between Americans and British.

Q: They hated you by extension.

Mr. Bond: That's right. That was a very strange feeling because as you walked along the streets, there'd be a cluster of people standing there, and you just felt their hate. Now, when you went into stores the people running them knew the difference. I mean, they'd recognize that the fellows in these uniforms were from the United States, and they had a lot of money. The fellows in those other uniforms were the English and they didn't have any. I'd say about half those storekeepers would try to convince you that they'd been to the world's fair in 1933 in Chicago.* Then they'd ask you where you were from and "Oh, boy, that's a nice area," and a special discount for that too.

But the average population didn't know the difference in nationalities, and they really hated us. I might say in the harbor in Trincomalee we always had armed guards patrolling the decks, because they'd had trouble with swimmers trying to attach explosives and things of that sort. The basic population was not pro-English.

Q: Another factor, I would think, is they didn't feel

---
*Officially known as the Century of Progress Exposition, it was one of the few such events during the Depression.

threatened by the war and didn't view you as protectors.

Mr. Bond: That's right. In fact, I think some Japanese companies had tea plantations in Ceylon prior to the war. They had much better working conditions than the average British plantation, so most of the Ceylonese felt that things would probably improve if the Japanese won. Even if they didn't have their own freedom or something like that, the conditions for them would improve.

The word "master" is a word we don't use much. Maybe in an old melodrama slave days, they'd use the word "master," but that was the word for white people in India and Ceylon. If you went to a railroad station, there were two waiting rooms: one had a sign that said "Masters," and the other one said "Natives." They were equal except that there were 10,000 natives trying to get in this one, and 15 or 20 whites in that one. And, you know, all the facilities were that way; there were "Masters" and "Natives." Some of the natives were very well-dressed, well-educated people, but they were not masters. That was a real cultural shock.

Q: You undoubtedly had to get your good uniforms better looking for these inspections and going on liberty than day-to-day work. Did you use the buckets for those too?

Mr. Bond: Oh, sure.

Q: Could you press them?

Mr. Bond: No. In the first place, you'd rinse your whites in regular fresh water to get the soap out. Then you'd rinse them in salt water, and the salt acted as a mild bleach, and it also gave it a little bit of body. Then you'd roll them tightly, and then you'd tie them just like they taught you in boot camp, and it worked out pretty well. And remember that a uniform is only supposed to be uniform. It doesn't mean it's supposed to be really sharp. The Marines were sharp; the Navy was uniform. Even if you could get a white uniform pressed, in that climate those creases would not stay sharp very long. And the way the Navy cut the trousers--of course, the creases are inside out along the side so you're not dealing with a crease down the front. The quartermasters always wore whites on watch and in port. So we were used to wearing our whites; a lot of the crew didn't, but we did.

Q: Well, you didn't have miracle detergents or automatic washing machines either. How did you get them clean?

Mr. Bond: You didn't let them get too dirty. That's the

secret of it. When you went on watch in whites, you wore them for that watch; you didn't wear them again. You washed them, and that way you could keep on top of it. You just didn't let them get dirty.

Q: How did you deal with the blues when you were in colder climates?

Mr. Bond: Well, you didn't wash your blues much. When we had colder climates, we could send the blues to the ship's cleaners because we weren't using them. Blues didn't show the soil, and you'd wear your undress blues, of course, most times. You only wore your dress blue jumper when you went ashore. And you could scrub your stripes on your dress blues without washing the whole uniform. Take a toothbrush and detergent or soap and work away at it. But, again, you didn't want to let them get too dirty, because if you did, you'd never get the yellow all the way out, and then you'd have to restripe them.

Q: Did you have to wear the uniform of the day for meals on board ship?

Mr. Bond: Well, the Saratoga was never really strong on the crew being in whites or blues. When we went in the yard in 1944 we got some fire-retardant paint, so the ship really did get painted pretty well again, the way it was before the war. But up until that time--all the time I was on it, basically--the ship was non-painted or just touched up, and there was a lot of rust. You wouldn't ask the crew to wear whites just generally aboard ship, because it was too dirty.

Q: And this was because of perceived fire hazard from the regular prewar paint?

Mr. Bond: That's right. But, you know, our uniform of the day was generally a dungaree shirt, a T-shirt, and dungaree trousers. You had to be in that uniform for meals or anything else. In port a lot of guys used to wear undress blues, but that wasn't really required. You could go through the chow line in dungarees. The guys that were working were still in dungarees.

Q: Were there pretty steady flight operations during this period in the Indian Ocean?

Mr. Bond: Oh, yes. When we were out, there were a lot of flight operations, and so we made several trips that you might say we trolled. We didn't get any strikes when we fished for Japanese. The first raid we had was in Sabang,

which is a small island immediately north of Sumatra.*
There was a large oil refinery at Sabang, and the channel
made a harbor. I recall we did have a fighter shot down
there, and the pilot got out, and it was in the harbor. An
English submarine was stationed there to pick up any pilots
that were shot down. She was at periscope depth, and the
crew saw that the Japanese were going to get out to the
pilot before the submarine got to him, so they surfaced and
ran in six miles on the surface to pick this guy up.**
They were under fire for the last several miles, anyway,
and then they got out and submerged.

The submarine that brought him out didn't get back for
a couple of weeks. When it did, the fighter squadron had
the entire crew of the submarine over for dinner in the
wardroom of the Saratoga. It was not a large sub, so there
were only about 60 fellows, and all the ice cream they
could eat. That always made a big impression on the
English because they had no ice cream. Most of them hadn't
had any since before the war.

Q: Well, the U.S. Navy was referred to as the "ice cream
navy."

Mr. Bond: That was a good description. In fact, our

---
*This raid by the two carriers was on 19 April 1944.
**As related in the article by Clark Reynolds, the pilot was Lieutenant (junior grade) Dale C. Klahn, flying an F6F, and the submarine was HMS Tactician.

destroyers didn't normally make ice cream unless they had maybe these little hand freezers in port or something. But we had a custom that whenever the plane guard destroyer picked up a pilot and returned him, we always sent them ice cream. And this word spread around the British fleet. So one day during air operations a plane came in very low, and the Saratoga's landing signal officer jumped for the net that was below him. But he jumped with such enthusiasm he jumped right over the net and into the water. The heavy cruiser London noted this. She was several thousand yards across the formation, but her men put the helm hard over, and just held down their whistle and came across that formation. Ships scurried to get out of the way, and the London picked up that guy. Now we had to furnish ice cream for 900 men, but we did. They got their ice cream.

Q: The other day you told me a story that's worth repeating about the race you had with the smaller ships.

Mr. Bond: Oh, that was after the raid on Sabang. As we were leaving the area, the Japanese were coming out, and it was getting dark. The enemy was sort of skirting around, and the Renown's admiral ordered, "Utmost speed."

Cassady saw that and said, "I never heard of that command before." But he got on the tube to the engineering officer and he said, "I want every last revolution you can get out of this thing." He said, "Somerville wants utmost speed, and I want to show him our utmost is better than theirs." We even walked away from our three destroyers. The commodore or acting commodore on one of the U.S. destroyers couldn't believe the speed the Saratoga was showing on the radar. He came out to the signal bridge and sent a message to Saratoga, "Interrogatory speed?"

So Cassady sent back, "Thirty-two knots and still building." Yeah, that was a kick.

Q: What did you get up to?

Mr. Bond: I don't think we got quite to 34, but the British destroyers would only do about 31 or 32. And the Renown only did 29, and Valiant and Queen Elizabeth, 25, so we were really moving away from everybody. Those U.S. destroyers were keeping pretty close, but they were laboring hard to do so, because they had a lot of miles on them too.

Q: You mentioned also the other day the eagerness with which the crew would watch flight operations topside sometimes.

Mr. Bond: Well, following a major battle, like at Rabaul,

when we knew there was a lot of action in the planes, the ship's superstructure and stack were just covered with men. A war correspondent mentioned to the air officer that he thought it was really touching for the men to be out there to see our heroes come home. The air officer said, "Bullshit! They're there to see the crackups because they know these planes have been shot up."

He says, "You don't mean that."

"You wait and see and watch them cheer for the crashes."

You know, you get sort of callous to the aircraft landings when they're happening all the time. And sometimes we'd be in situations where we were furnishing continual air cover, and planes were just coming and going all day long. Not big launches, but the planes kept moving on and off. After a while, you've seen them all, until there's something added like a plane that can't get its wheels down or tailhook down or something like that. Then that's going to be interesting, so you go watch it.

Q: Sort of like the mentality at an auto race. Watching laps alone is boring.

Mr. Bond: Yes, that's right. Yes, I think that's a good analogy, an auto race.

But, anyway, after we'd been there several months, it

came time to leave and go back to the States for overhaul. We had one other major operation, and that was on Surabaya in eastern Java.* In that one we came up on the south side of Java and the planes flew across the island to hit an aircraft assembly plant in Surabaya. We did lose one plane in that attack. The sad part about that was that it was the last action of Air Group 12 on the Saratoga. From there we proceeded back to Bremerton, and the air group went elsewhere. So the fact was that these guys had survived so much and for so long to do that.

We have mentioned Commander Caldwell; he became the ship's air officer at the end of 1943. The new air group commander was the fighter squadron commander, a very colorful character by the name of Jumping Joe Clifton, whom I'm sure you've heard of.**

Q: Yes.

Mr. Bond: Clifton was a fellow you didn't want to ring a bell around. He might come out swinging. I think the last reference I ever saw of Clifton was when he was captain of the Memphis Air Station, and he was the oldest active football player, because he was playing offensive guard for the air station team at the age of 53. It might not have

---
*This strike by Illustrious and Saratoga was on 17 May 1944.
**Commander Joseph C. Clifton, USN, Commander Carrier Air Group 12.

been real finesse football, but I'm sure it was very rough. He was then a four-striper. But Clifton was really something.

Q: What do you remember about him specifically?

Mr. Bond: Well, I remember that he had his ex-wives' names on the plane, both of them. Ada was the name we always saw. I forget what the one was on the port side of his plane because from the bridge Ada, on the starboard side, was the only one that was visible. And he wore an awful lot of cologne and whatever. He'd walk in the charthouse at night, with the doors dogged down, and it could be overpowering.

Q: You knew who it was.

Mr. Bond: Yes, you knew who it was. You didn't have to look up.

He was in the class of 1930 at the Naval Academy, and he knew he was too old to be reassigned as a fighter pilot.* He was doing everything he could to stay with that air group. They left the <u>Saratoga</u> in the Strait of Juan de Fuca in late June 1944 and landed at Naval Air

---

*Clifton was born 31 October 1908; in the spring of 1944 he was 35 years old

Station Sand Point in Seattle. So he finally had to give up when the ship came back.

Q: I interviewed a man who had been in a fighter squadron with him in the '30s as wing man. He said that really taught him to fly, because Clifton had a nervous tic that affected his flying, so the other pilot had to be very alert.* [Laughter]

Mr. Bond: I hadn't heard of that one, but I think he might have conquered the tic.

He was just a colorful, colorful character.

I remember we had a guy that wanted a transfer, and the commander asked him, "Why do you want a transfer?"

He said, "There's not enough character on this ship."

He said, "Characters? This whole ship's full of characters."

He said, "No, I said, 'character.'"

Q: Was Clifton an amusing guy to be around?

Mr. Bond: Well, yes. He never was surly or anything like that, but he was a hard-drinking guy that had a lot of zest for life. He was cut from the same cloth as that Marine

---

*The Naval Institute oral history of Captain David McCampbell, USN (Ret.), describes his flying with Clifton in Fighting Squadron Four of the USS Ranger (CV-4).

pilot, Pappy Boyington.* That is who I would say would be the same type of personality. Clifton would have made a good black sheep.

Q: Speaking of drinking, there are always these rumors about drinking on board aircraft carriers. Did you see that?

Mr. Bond: Well, a little bit. I knew where there were at least four stills aboard the ship, and I don't think I knew where all of them were. When they were arming the torpedo planes for Rabaul, they had a hard time finding 18 torpedoes that had a full charge of alcohol.** And we had 80-some torpedoes. But they hadn't been used and just been drained slowly over a period of time.

Q: What was the product of the stills?

Mr. Bond: The product of the stills was pretty pure alcohol. Most of the stills were to get the impurities out of the alcohol-based cleaning compounds that were used on the guns. You know, they were degreasing compounds. The cooks fermented and distilled fruit products to give them

---

*Major Gregory R. Boyington, USMC, commanded VMF-214, which was known as the Black Sheep Squadron. After being shot down and presumed lost in 1944, Boyington was awarded the Medal of Honor.
**Alcohol was used as fuel for the engines that propelled torpedoes toward their targets.

more punch.

The New Hebrides had a lot of lime plantations. So we had what we called a Tonga Collins. You'd get a bucket and squeeze all this lime juice and then put some alcohol in it. You couldn't taste the alcohol. You could usually get some ice aboard ship pretty easily if you were willing to share the product. But I wouldn't say there was a lot of chronic drinking. There was a lot more talk of it than actuality.

Q: Well, that's the fun part.

Mr. Bond: Yes, right. I do remember one time when we were in Trincomalee. It was a Sunday, and I had the afternoon watch. My relief lived down in the quartermaster storeroom in the anchor windlass room, and there was a hatch on the flight deck that led down there. In port it was open, and there was a ladder from the anchor windlass room up to the flight deck. So I thought, "Well, it's Sunday afternoon and hot and everything. I'd better make sure he's awake."

So I went down to check on him. A whole group of guys was in there drinking. They had this bucket of cold grapefruit juice, and someone said, "You want some?"

I said, "Sure." It was awfully hot, so I drank down a full Navy cup.

Then someone said, "There's just a little bit more. You can have the last of it."

It was almost another cup, and I drank that down. Then I said, "Well, I have to get back to the quarterdeck." So I went up the ladder onto the flight deck. I was walking towards the quarterdeck, and all of a sudden the superstructure moved. Then it started rotating. I just started going down, and I felt some hands under my armpits. The guys had followed me and caught me. I woke up in the darkened ready room of the superstructure on the flight deck. I never had an experience like that before. That just came right out of left field--Bong!

Q: After so long without it, I'm sure that it did quite a number on your system.

Mr. Bond: Well, I never drank very heavy anyway. But, you know, that was really a surprise because you couldn't taste anything in that cold grapefruit juice.

Q: Good that you were near the end of your watch.

Mr. Bond: Oh, yes. I hope they wouldn't have done that to me earlier in the watch.

Anyway, the day after this attack on Surabaya, we left the British fleet. We were steaming along in what I'd call sort of a task force formation, just doing 18 knots. Then we pulled ahead with our three destroyers and made a big turn. As we turned, why, the three destroyers strung out behind us. During this time we were pulling ahead, the British fleet had lined up in a single file, and we came down alongside them, steaming in the opposite direction. We came pretty close, maybe within a few hundred yards. It was pretty close for big ships to be passing. They had had all these flag hoists up, like "Good Luck," "Good Trip," all plain language through the international alphabet flags. The rails of all the ships were lined with their crews. As we went by, we'd get three cheers and we'd answer them. It was very, very impressive. I don't recall if the foreign ships were all in that formation, but there were 45 to 50 ships there, and they take up a long space in single file.

Q: It must have been miles.

Mr. Bond: Yes, it really was.

I know we were plenty hoarse by the time we got through, because they were only cheering four ships, and we were cheering 44, or whatever. But that really left us with a good feeling. I would say that we had very good relations with the British all the time we were there. I know a lot of men that have operated with the British fleet and didn't get along with them. They were very derogatory, said the ships were dirty and all that. We didn't find that at all. In fact, they were holystoning the decks in the Renown. Of course, that was the flag. I guess one reason for the goodwill was we weren't in a position where superior buying power meant anything. No matter how much money you had, you still needed a chit at the Royal Navy canteen to buy your bottle of beer.

Q: Where did the chits come from?

Mr. Bond: Well, you were issued the chits on the ship and you got four when you were going shore.

Although one day we were over at the Royal Navy canteen in Trincomalee, and there was a big Scotsman off the Valiant. I mean, he was a big man, probably 220, 230 pounds, about 6-4. He'd had his four bottles of beer, and I think he'd had somebody else's four bottles of beer. He went up to the bar or counter, and two little Ceylonese were working there. Neither one of them weighed 100 pounds, I'm sure, and they were both about five feet tall. He said, "I want a beer."

One of them said, "Ticket, money?"

He said, "I ain't got no tickets, and I ain't got no money." Then he picked one up in each hand and he shook them. And he said, "But I want a beer." So the Ceylonese each set up a couple bottles of beer, and he took the four bottles and he got on a chair and he said, "Look, mates, beer. No money, no tickets." With that, the Ceylonese left.

That place turned into a shambles. These guys just stormed the thing, liberated all this beer. That was a real brawl. We got out of there quick. That's when all the languages and cultures and everything clashed.

One thing, though, you found out the Canadians were on your side. They felt they were such an oppressed minority serving on the British ships that they'd rally to the Americans. And there were quite a few Canadians there. But, by golly, the next day they had the Royal Navy canteen open again.

But, as I said, we got along well with the British. There were always a lot of British visiting the ship. They found out our cigarettes were tax free. Whenever a boat went from A to B, they went, A, to Saratoga, to B, so they could go by and buy some cigarettes.

Q: It wasn't a straight line?

Mr. Bond: No, in fact, frequently very, very circuitous. Of course, there was a lot of going back and forth for movies. I watched many movies on the Valiant. On the Valiant they showed the movies on the boat deck, and you'd sit around where the boat cradles were, and the movie screen was up against the superstructure. They didn't have two projectors, so at the end of the reel, they had to change reels and thread it through, and the guys would sing. I've never seen that in the American Navy.

Of course, the British ran on four meals a day: breakfast, lunch, tea, and supper. My friend Lenny came over one day for dinner and a movie. We had dinner about 4:30 in the afternoon, and he said, "Gosh, you guys have more for tea than we have for supper."

I said, "You'd better load up. This is the end. There ain't no more."

"No?"

Q: He thought that was tea.

Mr. Bond: He thought that was tea. In the British Navy, a ship only served biscuits and tea for tea, and then you furnished your own food. You could buy things at the ship's service. So they had jams, cheese, tinned meat, or something like that. But they provided that themselves. Most of them still ate in table messes in their living areas. Of course, in the British Navy they all were in hammocks. There were no bunks for enlisted men, or, as they called them, ratings.

Another thing I noticed on the *Valiant* were all the

rifles, just racks of rifles in the passageways. It was obvious there were a lot more rifles than there were Marines, so said, "Whose rifles are these?"

Someone said, "They're ours." I found out that every British sailor had a rifle.

I said, "What's that for?"

He said, "For landing parties."

I said, "Do you put any men ashore?"

Yes, they did. In North Africa a number of times. Lenny didn't have a rifle as a signalman, but he had so darn much to carry that I don't see how a man could carry everything: signal lamps and wet-cell batteries and things of that sort. But they actually did supplement the landing forces with Navy troops in World War II. It has been a long time since the American Navy did that.

Q: How did the British movies compare with the American ones that you were used to seeing?

Mr. Bond: Well, basically, they were about the same movies. They had a lot of American movies. Some were British movies that I saw after the war in the States. One I remember starred Charles Laughton, where he was an Australian boxer in The Man from Down Under. I can't remember much of the movie, but I remember seeing it in the States after the war. They were about the same.

Q: Did the British send any liaison people to the Saratoga for communications or tactical purposes?

Mr. Bond: No one of officer rank; the only ones they sent were people to facilitate visual signaling and radio communication. We also picked up an English signalman when we got to Trincomalee. So we had the Australian and English, and the radio gang had about six or eight Aussies and English there, but they didn't have any officers aboard. Those guys got a big kick out of serving on the Saratoga, and especially Australians because they were on there for about four months. But they had a heck of a time getting used to sleeping in bunks, oddly enough. They preferred their hammocks.

I became pretty close friends with Larry Ennis, the Aussie we had. In fact, we swapped hats. I still have his hat at home. When we came back to Fremantle for a few days on our way back home, I visited his family up in Perth, which is really a beautiful city. It's a fairly new city; the old town is Fremantle. When the Australians moved to build Perth, they knew they were laying out a big city and did a nice job.

I was pretty impressed with Australia. In fact, after I got out of college I think I probably would have been tempted to go to Australia, except that at that time they had a socialist government, which ended it for me. I mean, I wouldn't have gone there. But they had a funny slant too. They were awfully afraid of putting on airs or acting important. They had such a negative viewpoint towards anyone in a position of influence or authority or anything else, that I just thought that wasn't really very healthy, and I wouldn't want to raise a family in it.

Other than that, I enjoyed the Aussies, and I enjoyed Australia. When we came back around, we also visited Sydney for a while. And I remember the place where we moored. The pier was on one side, and then on the other side was a park, a peninsula that came out. There were girls over in the park trying to strike up conversations by semaphore. When that happened, you had the feeling that the Navy had been there several times before.

Q: Yes.

Mr. Bond: But we had about three or four days, about two liberties in Sydney, and then we left for the States.

Q: Well, they're certainly a very open and friendly people.

Mr. Bond: Oh, yes. I'll tell you the reason the girls liked the Americans so much. Before the war, if an Aussie fellow had some money, he called up some friends of his and they went out drinking. If he was flat broke, he called up a girlfriend and they went out walking. The American sailor was willing to spend the money on the girl, and that influenced her quite a bit. So I think the Aussie men had to change their system after that. We destroyed their way of life.

When we came back to the States for this yard period, we found out that the crew was going to be in the Fourth of July parade in Seattle. Somebody volunteered us. So the executive officer felt the Marines ought to sharpen up the sailors on their drill. The flight deck was pretty open during our transit to the United States, because we weren't flying any aircraft. There was no combat air patrol or antisubmarine patrol. Of course, these Marines really didn't have any authority over us. Most of us outranked them. You never saw such frustrated people in your life as those Marines, because you would have sworn that the sailors in the crew didn't know their right from their left or they couldn't count over three or whatever.

Q: Deliberately not.

Mr. Bond: Oh, yes, deliberately. I got on the first leave party, so I happened to be away during the parade, but I understand the crew did very well in it.

Q: What was your rate by then?

Mr. Bond: I was a third class.

Q: When did you get rated?

Mr. Bond: I think I was rated about February of '44.

Q: Did you have to take a test, or how did you demonstrate your proficiency?

Mr. Bond: On the *Saratoga*, especially for a right-arm rate, you had to take three tests. The first was a qualifications exam, which was out of the Bureau of Naval Personnel. That was a standard test with true-or-false and multiple-choice questions. Then you took a practical exam, which was made up by your division officer. Then you took an A to N exam, petty officer's exam, which also came out of the Bureau of Personnel. After those three tests, you took the final exam, and the total average had to be over 3.5.

Q: What did the final exam consist of?

Mr. Bond: Well, in our case, those were mostly essay

questions. And they were pretty well in depth. Commander Beebe made them up. The practical exam, of course, would be on things that were in our duties, and we actually demonstrated skills that would be at the petty officer level that we were going up for.

Q: Since you had been doing it every day for a year, that was second nature.

Mr. Bond: Third class was easy, because that really was about the things that you were doing all the time. But when you were going for second class, they'd have you doing sun lines and azimuths, and then's when you'd get into demonstrating the ability to compensate the compass and things of this sort. That's also where the signaling came in. Then the final exams were mostly essay examinations and a lot on charts and ship handling. On the petty officer's exam, A to N, those were more military things.

Q: Was The Bluejackets' Manual a useful source on those?

Mr. Bond: Yes, that was the primary study medium there. And that became sort of repetitious as you went up in rate. You couldn't elaborate a whole lot more on that.

During my time on the ship, we never increased our complement of petty officers, so there would be two or three guys taking the exam for one opening. When I went for second class in the Saratoga, I was going against a guy by the name of Hugo Brandt.* He and I were very similar, and it was very close. I think Hugo had a 3.86 cumulative, and I had 3.83 or 3.82, or something like that. So for all those exams, I think it really was only a difference of a question or two in the whole thing.

Q: He got it and you didn't.

Mr. Bond: Yes, he got the second class and I got the transfer. This was the first second class opening in 13 months, and there was also a transfer for a third class. So I said, "Well, if I lose, I'll take the transfer."

And he said, "If I lose, I'll take the transfer." So we took the exams, and that's the way it worked.

Q: Those were pretty impressive scores.

Mr. Bond: Well, yes, but if you got by the qualifications and you were interested, you knew a lot. That was all we talked about; it was our trade, so to speak. Our main topic of conversation when we were playing cards or something like that was experiences of different ships, characteristics, ship handling, charts, sailing directions.

───────────
*Quartermaster Third Class Wilbert Hugo Brandt, USN.

We read the coast pilots and sailing directions for fun because we were that interested in them. We'd get into all kinds of discussions. I was looking at the coast pilot that ran from Cape May, New Jersey, to somewhere south of there, and I said, "Did you know . . . ?" And then I'd start telling about it. Then somebody who had been there and operated there would add something else. You just got this all the time.

Q: You'd be over in the Indian Ocean talking about Cape May?

Mr. Bond: Oh, sure. Another topic of conversation was, "Did you know that the Norwegian buoy system is different running north and south than it is running east and west?"* Because of all the islands and fjords, it was very important that the colors would indicate which way you're going and stuff like that, you know. We heard about that because somebody was correcting charts of Europe.

Q: Sounds almost like one of those sports trivia contests.

Mr. Bond: Oh, God, if we had had trivia then, we'd have really been good at it. But, as I said, we maintained the full outpouring of the Hydrographic Office. So each

---
*This is no longer the case because of a subsequent international agreement on buoys.

quartermaster would be assigned certain portfolios of charts to keep up to date. It might be a portfolio that had absolutely nothing to do with any place you'd been, such as northern Europe. Now, I never did have to keep up Scandinavia. But I remember how surprised we were that we were getting notices to mariners telling about beacons and buoys being down on the German river system and things like that. You wondered how in the world they came out with all that sort of stuff. But, you know, there were Swedish ships, I guess, and other neutrals going in there, so the Germans had to make that information available.

But it was an unusual group, I feel, and it wasn't just in that. There were just so many guys that had been in the Navy a long time, and they inculcated this into the newer people. And the newer guys joined the culture that was already there. But the atmosphere on that ship was that this was your profession, and you were interested in it. And, of course, we discussed and cussed all kinds of ships and classes and analyzed them, and talked about the British and French. We had guys that in peacetime had visited German ships and fellows that had been on French ships, which truly were filthy. We were all very interested in that sort of thing.

Q: It was part of the in-culture, and you wanted to belong

to that group.

Mr. Bond: Sure. If you weren't interested in that, you just wouldn't have had anything in common with that group. I don't know what you'd have done. You would have gotten transferred, I guess. And yet the signalmen were a lot the same way. We had a compartment full of fire controlmen aft of us, and they were gung ho about the same thing. Now, when we stood watch in steering aft, there was a machinist's mate that also was there, and that was sort of fun because you got to meet someone from a different culture. That was our only real contact with the engineering department or the snipes. We got acquainted with them. That machinist's mate and the bridge electrician were about the only ones we really knew.

Incidentally, even though we didn't have a steering wheel on the bridge, there _was_ a wheel down in steering aft, and that wheel activated the hydraulic pumps. The rudder in the Saratoga was controlled by rams that were about 30 inches in diameter, I guess. There were two of them in these hydraulic cylinders. An awful lot of officers of the deck in just general steaming would transfer the steering down to the steering aft just for practice and make sure you weren't sleeping or something. Since we were frequently zigzagging, it wasn't just maintaining the ship on course. I don't remember how many revolutions it took to change that rudder one degree, but I know you just spun it and spun it and spun it in order to get that rudder moving. Because here you were by hand pumping the oil to move those big rams, and you had to have a lot of mechanical advantage with that pump to do it. Then you'd just about get steadied up and it'd be time to change course again.

Q: That would be tough if you had to maneuver while under attack.

Mr. Bond: Oh, yes. Incidentally, the same guy was in steering aft both times the ship was torpedoed.* After the second time the division officer promised him he'd never have steering aft as a general quarters assignment again.

Q: And not just for his own protection.

Mr. Bond: Right. You know the Saratoga also had an armored deck, and the scuttle and hatch on that armored deck was jammed by the second torpedoing, and they couldn't get it open for a couple of hours. He really had a traumatic experience the second time getting out of there.

---
*On 11 January 1942 the Saratoga was torpedoed by the Japanese submarine I-16 while in the vicinity of Hawaii. On 31 August 1942 the ship was torpedoed by the submarine I-26 during the Guadalcanal operation.

One time they showed a movie called <u>Arsenic and Old Lace</u> aboard the ship. Of course, Cary Grant, Boris Karloff, and Peter Lorre were in it. There was also a guy that played the crazy uncle who thought he was Teddy Roosevelt and was digging the Panama Canal. You know, he'd go down in the basement when he was burying the aunts' victims. After we'd seen that movie, whenever we were going down to steering aft we always said, "Well, we're going to go down and dig another lock in the Panama Canal." You'd also hear guys yell, "Charge." Because this crazy uncle always went up the stairs like Roosevelt up San Juan Hill.*

But that was sort of a strange deal going back then.

Q: You were talking about going on leave from Bremerton. Did you go to California again?

Mr. Bond: No, when we got into Bremerton I got a letter from my mother saying that she was going back to Milwaukee. And, as you recall, I like to give surprises. I was in the first leave party, so when I found out she was in Milwaukee, I just went to Milwaukee.

I took the train. There wasn't any way I could get an airline ticket. I mean, if I had, I would have been days

---

*San Juan Hill in Cuba was the site of a noted charge by Theodore Roosevelt and his Rough Riders during the Spanish-American War of 1898.

after the train arrived. I went all the way to Milwaukee in the smoking lounge of the car. There weren't any seats left, but they let me buy a ticket to sit there, and that was sort of uncomfortable. After I got into Milwaukee, I took the streetcar out to where my aunt and uncle lived and my mother was staying. I'd been there a lot, and I knew where it was. When the streetcar pulled away after I got off, I looked across the street, and there was my mother waiting for a streetcar going downtown. She looked startled, because she hadn't known where in the world I was. As far as she was concerned, I was out in the Pacific. That was one surprise that was really a surprise.

That was a very good leave, to be in Milwaukee in July of 1944. It was very hard for a serviceman to spend any money in Milwaukee. There was no bases around there. A few guys would come up from Great Lakes, but basically, they went to Chicago.* The ones that did only came on the weekends.

Q: Was the Schroeder Hotel one of your hangouts there?

Mr. Bond: Yes, I'd been to the Schroeder a number of times

---

*Great Lakes, Illinois, north of Chicago on the shore of Lake Michigan, was the site of a vast naval training station. Among other things, it was one of the Navy's two principal recruit training commands at the time. The other was the one Bond went through in San Diego.

and the Pfister. My grandmother was pastry chef at the Pfister Hotel when she was alive. And my uncle was a member of the downtown Elks Club, which had a very good athletic facility, big pool and basketball courts. So I spent a lot of time there.

Q: And Milwaukee was also very hospitable through the USO for the servicemen.*

Mr. Bond: Yes, you could get tickets for shows or anything else. Even on the streetcar, you couldn't spend money. Theoretically, the servicemen rode free from something like 9:00 to 4:00. But I got on during the times when you were supposed to pay, and they still wouldn't take my money. They had enough of a loophole that they just didn't take it. It was really sort of neat to be treated that way for a while.

Then, of course, I did fly back to the West Coast because I could make my reservations. I flew to Oakland and visited some of my friends. I didn't go down to Los Angeles at all. I did go on a flight that went to Seattle, and I sat next to Ty Cobb.** A man who was a friend of my

---

*USO--United Service Organization, a charitable outfit that had centers in many cities to provide recreation for servicemen. The USO also sponsored troupes of entertainers who traveled to the world's various war theaters.
**Tyrus R. Cobb was one of the original members of the Baseball Hall of Fame, elected in 1936. He played for many years for the Detroit Tigers and compiled the highest lifetime batting average in major league history, .367.

mother's there in Milwaukee had written a book about the World Series since 1903 and had given me a copy. I was reading this on the plane very avidly. The fellow next to me asked me if I liked baseball. I said yes, I sure did. When he got off at Portland, the stewardess came up and asked me, "Did you get his autograph?"

I said, "Who?"

She said, "Well, you've been sitting next to Ty Cobb all the way from Oakland to Portland reading a baseball book. I thought you might have gotten it." I was just shocked to find that out. I was sure that at the time I was sitting next to him I'd read the part that had a full-page picture of him.

Then I got back to the <u>Saratoga</u>, and they were doing a lot of extensive work inside, in the hangar deck and the torpedo loft and all. Our compartment was right on the other side of the bulkhead, so the compartment wasn't livable. Across the inlet at Port Orchard they had some housing for married men. The houses were up over the little hill and woods; they were little square buildings with a partition that made sort of a bedroom and then the L-shaped little kitchen and dining room. The houses were big enough for a man and wife and maybe a baby to stay. So they put ten of us in one.

It was more darn fun because it was so different from the ship. They all had wood stoves, and we got the job of delivering the wood to the locations around there and picking up the garbage. And that was more fun. We just lived in dungarees. We'd go down to the little dinky town of Port Orchard in our dungarees, go down for a beer in the evening or something. We were out there for about three weeks and had more fun doing that. We didn't even go over to Seattle or anything you would call a regular liberty. We also made money there, because we were in big demand as babysitters.

And, you know, the married people got sort of a kick out of us. Actually, about 30 of us were over there, three houses full.

Q: How did you get back and forth to the ship?

Mr. Bond: Well, you could walk down to Port Orchard. They had a motor launch that went right across to the Navy yard. Really, it was only the equivalent of walking a couple or three blocks.

Q: Did you go on liberty at all in Bremerton itself?

Mr. Bond: Sometimes. On Second Avenue in Bremerton was a bar called The Service Club. The guy who ran the bar was an old shipmate of our chief. Any of us could always go into The Service Club and have a couple of beers if we were broke. Another thing was that if you ever needed any uniform parts, people were always leaving parts of uniforms in his place, and he had quite a lucky bag for you to go through if you needed hats or jumpers or anything like that. So usually we'd go over to The Service Club, and we got to know the people there and maybe have a couple of beers and go to a show. There was a bowling alley up about Sixth Avenue. And then the Craven Center, the ship's service in the Navy yard, was an outstanding service center. It was very good.

Q: What did it have for recreation?

Mr. Bond: Oh, it had ping-pong; it had bowling; it had the swimming pool; it had pool tables; it had a movie there. I'm trying to think; it might have even had two movies. It had a library, reading room. It was really a pretty good place, and probably better than anything you could dig up in Seattle or Bremerton.

Q: Certainly more convenient.

Mr. Bond: And more convenient. That's right. And they sold beer there, so you could have a couple beers. That's where you went when you got tired of going to Seattle, which, after all, is a 50-minute ferry ride. You got to see a little bit of Seattle and that was enough.

I remember one time we went to Seattle, and I really had the hiccups bad while standing in line at the box office at a movie. The guy ahead of me said, "Do you want to get rid of those hiccups?"

I said, "Yeah, I sure do."

He said, "Are you willing to pay a dollar to get rid of them?"

I said, "Well, I think so."

He said, "I'll bet you a dollar you can't hiccup again."

And I couldn't hiccup again. [Laughter] So that was an educational trip. But I liked seafood, and every once in a while we'd go over to Seattle for some good seafood.

Q: How did you spend your working days there in the yard?

Mr. Bond: Well, of course, we were mostly standing watch. When we were living over at Port Orchard, we'd only stand watch every fourth day. But then when we'd come back to the ship we would take two six-hour watches a day. Two of us would split the day. So that would maximize our usefulness and cut down on the commuting. The quartermasters didn't have a whole lot to do in port except

Bond #2 - 194

keep up the charts and that sort of thing. We took a lot of the charts over to Port Orchard with us, too, and did it over there, because they sure weren't being used on the ship.

Q: After a while did you get eager to go back to sea again?

Mr. Bond: I think so. I think we were ready by the time the second leave party got back. By then the shipyard had built all those sponsons and put on all those 40-millimeter guns. Also, we got two catapults. I had mentioned we didn't have a catapult. Before the war somebody got the idea that it might be interesting if they could launch or recover aircraft at either end of the ship. Now, if your flight deck was bombed, you certainly weren't going to launch any aircraft. But if you had aircraft out, then you could recover them. So they put arresting gear in the bow of the Saratoga, and to do that, they took out the catapults. So from the beginning of the war until '44 the ship did not have any catapults. Then we got the catapults back.

We left Bremerton about the middle of September. Basically my leave was the month of July. I think I came back the 29th or something like that. Then the next leave party went immediately. So the second leave party was back just a fairly short time before we left.

After we got under way, the Saratoga made a speed run down the Strait of Juan de Fuca, and she did 34.7 knots. For a ship of that age, one which was about 15% overweight from its design speed, that was pretty remarkable.* But they always explained to me that because of the fact that it was electric drive, the boilers and turbines were never under maximum strain. The electric generators maxed out before the turbines did. Those ships had terrific sustaining power, and that's why the Lexington was able to go to Pearl Harbor from San Francisco in about 72 hours when she was searching for Amelia Earhart.** It was a sustaining power, and very frequently high-speed steam operation becomes less efficient as the machinery heats up and all. You begin to lose a little bit of efficiency. But, anyway, we were pretty proud of that because that was different than the day when morale went down.

Q: You also had a clean bottom right out of the yard.

Mr. Bond: Oh, yes, sure we did. There's no question that helped a lot too.

---

*The Saratoga was then nearly 17 years old, having been commissioned in November 1927.
**Amelia Earhart (1898-1937) became the first woman to fly across the Atlantic Ocean on 17 June 1928. She and her copilot/navigator Fred Noonan were lost in July 1937 during the course of an attempted around-the-world flight.

Q: Where did the ship wind up after those sea trials?

Mr. Bond: Well, then we went on out to Pearl Harbor, and this is where we had some trouble with this new high-speed elevator. We went into a routine of going out on Monday and coming back in on Friday. Various air groups in the area would use the Saratoga for practice landings and qualify pilots for night operations. The yard workers would work on the elevator machinery, and these pilots would just land, taxi forward, and take off.

Q: Did you have a new air group yet?

Mr. Bond: No, we didn't have a new air group yet. And so finally they got the elevator working. We had had only one usable elevator from the time the F6Fs came aboard. We had two, but the after elevator wasn't big enough to handle the F6F. It would handle an F4F. The planes got too large, so then the forward elevator was the only one, which wasn't a really good arrangement.

We were in the Hawaii area into early 1945 on this night training mission. In late January we got a new air group and left for Ulithi.*

Q: So, except for the Marshalls, you had pretty much

---

*Night Air Group 53.

missed the rest of the central Pacific campaign after that.

Mr. Bond: Yes, we really had. Nothing about the Philippines or the Marianas. Never got to the Marianas until I got out on the PCE(R), and that was Tinian.

Anyway, we went out there, and they were forming up a night task group.* Just like when we were in the Indian Ocean, we didn't have an admiral aboard. Sherman had left at the end of '43, after the Gilberts. He'd been aboard so long that his flag group seemed just like the ship's company. It was sort of a shock to see those guys go. And it reminds you that it wasn't like the air group. You know, the air group mechanics and everything were just like ship's company. And up and away they go.

So in early '45 we went up in and were in those first carrier raids on Japan. That was really a different kind of operating, really big fleet operating. We had so darn many ships that it was just overwhelming. At that time there was a lot of straight operating and going up, and we'd hit targets there in Japan. I forget how many carriers were in those huge raids.

And then we were detached to provide air cover at Iwo

---

*In early 1945, the Saratoga and Enterprise (CV-6), the two remaining prewar carriers, formed Task Group 58.5 for night operations. The task group commander was Rear Admiral Matthias B. Gardner, USN, embarked in the Enterprise.

Jima. That's where we were bombed.*

Q: Do you think the Saratoga was in this night task group because her operating characteristics were different from the Essex class?

Mr. Bond: I wouldn't be surprised. I really wouldn't. The Saratoga just really didn't fit. Now, we fit with the British fine, because we were so much faster in our operations. We couldn't overcome the speed of operations for the Essex class, even though they had a larger air group. We just really didn't fit. There was always this problem of launching aircraft, turning out of the wind after launching most of the planes. We'd end up with about 18 fighters down below on the hangar deck. We'd bring them up, warm them up, go back into the wind.

If you were in an operation like around the Marshalls or Eniwetok and those, where there's an ongoing operation with small sorties coming and going over all day long, it probably didn't mean very much there. Because if you're going to launch eight, ten planes, we could do that fine. But I wouldn't be surprised if the Saratoga's age got us the separate assignments. I never thought of it quite like that. I wouldn't be surprised if that was the reason.

---

*For an account of the kamikaze attacks on the Saratoga on 21 February 1945, see Samuel Eliot Morison, Volume XIV of United States Naval Operations in World War II (Boston: Little, Brown, 1960), pages 52-54.

Q: Your tactical diameter might have been a problem too.

Mr. Bond: And the tactical diameter was a problem. It wasn't so much a problem for us. It was a problem for everybody else.

Q: That's right.

Mr. Bond: We couldn't change it. Yes, that could very well be. We were just better used in a small formation, either a single carrier, maybe ourselves and a light carrier, something of that sort.

Q: What do you remember about the Iwo Jima tragedy?

Mr. Bond: Well, the main thing I remember about that was that I wasn't on watch. We were down in the berthing compartment, and the guns started firing. That was extremely strange. Right then, of course, they called for general quarters. At that time my general quarters station was in after control, which was at the aft end of the stack. I didn't really like it too much because there wasn't anything to do. We were only a standby station. But, anyway, the executive officer was back there, and so I went there, and it just was unbelievable.

Q: Did the first enemy plane hit before you got to your GQ station?

Mr. Bond: No, we were at GQ before the first actual hit.

Q: How much did you see of it?

Mr. Bond: Well, I saw quite a bit. We took one plane on the starboard side that actually was glancing. But it hit next to that 40-millimeter sponson in the starboard boat pocket. That caused a lot of damage. Then the flames on the after end of the flight deck were pretty visible. We couldn't see very much of the bow from where we were.

Q: I guess you were blocked off by the stack.

Mr. Bond: Yes, and sort of out on the wings. You could get a little idea. But the fire was really the outstanding memory that I have of that thing--almost to the point where the rest of it is a side issue. I think all of us felt the danger to the ship was from the fire. But they got it under control, and, of course, the fire was on the hangar deck. They were fueling planes down there, and that's what really fueled the fire. I can't think of that hangar deck officer's name. He used to stand officer of the deck watches. He was really a well-liked guy, and he was lost.*

After it was over, we went into Eniwetok.

Q: I think you told me also there was some criticism or questioning of why the ship wasn't at general quarters beforehand.

Mr. Bond: Yes, there definitely was, and the crew really was upset about that. Moebus never, never achieved the position that Cassady had with the crew. He was sort of a quiet guy and didn't interact really.

Q: Captain Moebus had a hard act to follow.

Mr. Bond: Well, yes, he did. But he just wasn't the seaman, we didn't think, that Cassady was. He was more of a flier than a ship's officer.

Q: Did you have the feeling that he didn't realize these were enemy planes?

Mr. Bond: Oh, yes, that was it. We felt that he had made a complete miscalculation. I read something about a year

---

*According to the Saratoga action report of 7 March 1945, the kamikaze attacks on the ship resulted in a total of 123 men killed and missing and 192 wounded.

later, shortly before I left the service. The war was over, but this article was about miscalculations and all, and you could tell they were talking about the Saratoga incident. The radar had identified the planes as friendly. What the article basically said is when you have well-trained lookouts and they identify something as enemy, that's the thing to believe and not a technical instrument.

Q: That's curious about the radar. You'd think, if anything, it'd be the opposite because the Japanese wouldn't be flashing an IFF signal.

Mr. Bond: Well, several times we had to change the IFF code because the Japanese had it.

Q: Oh, so they were flashing the IFF?

Mr. Bond: That's what I understand: the radar showed an IFF.

Anyhow, the gist of it was if you're going to make an error, you're much better making an error by sending your crew to general quarters and being ready for something that turns out to be a false alarm than to have it the other way around.

Q: Err on the side of caution.

Mr. Bond: Yes, err on the side of caution.

Q: Was there some kind of a mass burial service for the men who were killed?

Mr. Bond: Yes, and that was a very moving service. Now, we'd buried a number of men at sea. All the other ones that I saw buried at sea were crew members from the planes. This was the first time when I was on the ship the crew had sustained any deaths. Even in the second torpedoing there wasn't anybody killed. The initial torpedoing was the only other case of men from the ship's company being killed in action.

Q: And you didn't lose just some when the kamikaze hit; you lost a lot.

Mr. Bond: Yes, that was a lot. And, of course, that makes a big impact on you. The way we did it, I guess, was the standard Navy way. They sewed them up in canvas and put a 5-inch projectile between each man's feet in the age-old fashion of a burial at sea. That particular service is straight out of the Anglican prayer book, and I happen to be an Episcopalian. The new prayer book doesn't have it quite that way. The old one had the burial-at-sea service set aside by itself. Now, they interchange parts of it.

Now, as far as our particular group, no quartermaster was hurt or killed. So we didn't have any trauma like that. We found out, too, the group was beginning to break up a little bit. Because we'd lost to transfers a number of guys who'd gone to the Hancock and the Bon Homme Richard and a couple of others.

Q: Does a crew get more apprehensive after something like that? If they lose confidence in the captain, do they have more concern?

Mr. Bond: Well, I think so, but the Saratoga never returned to action after that. I visited aboard her in Pearl Harbor about the first week in June after I had been transferred to the PCE(R). One electrician explained to me that the Saratoga was just one big short circuit. Mechanically down below it ran fine, but it was just like the whole thing was warped. But it was sort of good to see the ship, because it really was repaired and restored. When I went aboard we'd have never guessed four months before it had that terrific damage and fire.

Q: But essentially, except for those few raids on Japan you described, she didn't do much of anything after the Indian Ocean operation.

Mr. Bond: That's right, because we had a long trip back to Bremerton, the yard period, which was two and a half months, and coming out and having all that problem with that elevator. So we went eight months without really doing anything active except for training.

Q: Well, just reflect, though, on that short period of two years when you reported aboard in 1943, you and the Enterprise were holding the line in the Pacific. And now there were so many carriers that the Saratoga didn't make a difference.

Mr. Bond: That's right. It completely, completely changed. There were actually two wars. If you came in after, let's say, January 1, 1944, you had a completely different experience and viewpoint than those that were before, because it really was two different operations.

I wasn't part of the one where we truly were losing and getting chased all over the place. I was part of the holding the line. We just felt that we were hanging on by our fingernails and didn't know what was going on. Today it's hard to believe that you could be part of the Navy and know so little about what's happening back in the States and other places. We were really in sort of an independent unit. And, of course, in those wartime conditions it wasn't on the daily news or the newspaper. So, as I said that day we were in the Gilberts and saw 13 carriers in one day was an awesome, awesome day. Now, sure, four or five of those were light carriers and all. But to think that you're like a passenger pigeon and then you run into a whole flock, you know, is pretty surprising.

Q: Did you feel a sense of disappointment after this competition with the other quartermaster that you were having to leave the ship?

Mr. Bond: No, not really, because I also wanted to get back on a destroyer then. I guess I've always felt--and I do to this day--that the most exciting things are still to come. I look forward to doing new things and seeing new places, so I looked forward to being on another ship. Now, if I'd gotten second class, that would have been fine, but I didn't, so I'd take the transfer and see if I could do something else.

I went aboard a transport at Eniwetok and rode to Treasure Island on the West Coast.* This ship was a converted French passenger liner. The U.S. Navy commandeered it at the beginning of the war. Of course, we were going in the opposite direction from the main thrust

---

*Treasure Island is a man-made island near San Francisco's Yerba Buena Island. It was the site of the 1939-40 Golden Gate International Exposition and then was taken over by the Navy for use as an administrative facility.

of the war, so there weren't a whole lot of us going back. But they gave us a feeling of it because they crammed us all into one living area, so we were just as crowded as if the ship had been full. But we did have three meals a day, and didn't have all the crowding to get in the mess hall and stuff.

I will say that the receiving stations were getting pretty good at handling people in those days. You got back to Treasure Island, and you went on leave immediately. I mean, it was just like the next day. I went down to Los Angeles that time, had 30-day leave, and then came back to Treasure Island.

Q: Did you have any say at all in what your next assignment would be?

Mr. Bond: Well, when I got back from leave, I had some interviews. I kept stressing that I was really qualified for small ships. When you're on a carrier, you forget there are ships smaller than a destroyer. You're really stressing this smallness of the ship, thinking that there's carriers, battleships, heavy cruisers, light cruisers, and destroyers. So, by God, they put up the list, and I was transferred to small craft training center in Miami. Then I took one long train ride from San Francisco to Miami.

Q: Did servicemen on transfer official orders have priority over guys on leave in getting transportation?

Mr. Bond: Well, we had a draft, and we almost filled two cars. There was a chief petty officer in charge, and he said, "You guys are all grown up, and you're veterans and I don't need to explain anything to you. But you're not on leave; you're not on liberty; you're on duty. I'm going to count you when we get to Miami. If you're not here, you're a deserter. But other than that, I'm not going to worry about you." So he didn't.

Q: These were essentially like chartered train cars.

Mr. Bond: Yes, that's exactly like what they were. And, you know, one night I got up. We started out and went to Pocatello, Idaho, where they took our two cars off the train they were attached to. This was while we were sleeping. I got up in the early morning to go to the head, which was up in the front of the car. When I looked out the front window, there was a boxcar ahead of us. So we were on a freight train from whatever that junction point was into Salt Lake. So we were attached to several trains.

I remember one thing on that trip. In Nebraska the law was they couldn't sell liquor while a train was in town. So we drew straws, and one guy got left behind. He went and bought some liquor and then hitchhiked ahead and met us at the next town. It wasn't hard either. That showed you what an "express" we were with.

We went through Chicago and down to Miami, which was a far different place than it is today, very much smaller. On the waterfront the municipal pier was about the only pier there. The Navy had some classrooms built on the pier, but it was still used by this little steamship company that ran between Miami and Nassau. If you were around, you helped handle the lines to tie this guy up.

We lived in hotels along Biscayne Boulevard. I was at the McAlister Hotel, which was at the corner of Biscayne and Flagler, which has got to be the crossroads of Miami. Then the next hotel was the Everglades, I think, and that was pretty much officers. Then came the Alcazar, which was used for some classes, and most of the foreign sailors were there, including the Russians. And that was sort of fun. You always had to check them out at least once. The Russians, I think, were on the sixth deck. You just had to punch six to go up there. The door would open, and you'd see a Russian standing in front of you. He must have been standing about six inches from the door all the time. When the door opened, there he was with a rifle at port arms, barring your way.

We had a lot of South Americans, like the Venezuelans.

We were really tough on military discipline. The command really wanted you to salute officers. But I'll tell you, a Venezuelan petty officer had more braid than an admiral's aide. After you saluted a couple of times, you found out this guy was a just petty officer. We also had Chinese there. We were providing them with submarine chasers.

I was in the signal school there in Miami. The signal school was from the balcony on the office of our hotel across to the park, Biscayne Park. We would lie out in the park and take down the code.

Q: This was really tough duty you were on.

Mr. Bond: Oh, yes. We were really impressed by how tough this was.

I remember one guy in the class had a deaf relative, so he knew sign language. We began practicing that so we could talk in class. Then it really came in handy in another way. There was a nice-looking girl that was in the park one day, and we were trying to get acquainted with her. We weren't making any headway--talk about being snubbed--and all of a sudden this guy realized she was deaf. So then he used the sign language, and she was overwhelmed. Then she found out that all three of us knew it, and we all dated her. She was really a nice gal and came from a family where everybody used sign language. She really didn't realize how dependent she was on her supporting group. When she got down there, she was really very unhappy and lonely and had a hard time communicating. So maybe we helped her too.

So then we were constantly being assigned to crews. After I'd been there, oh, only about a week or two, I got assigned to the nucleus crew for this PCE(R). It was to be commissioned about the first of May, so about the first part of April we went up to Chicago and picked it up. I was a plank owner.

Q: What was the name of the ship?

Mr. Bond: PCE(R)-858.

Q: Didn't have a name then?

Mr. Bond: Well, we gave it a name. It was the "Be-No" because they were always passing the word, "There will be no liberty today. There will be no this. There will be no that."

The ship was built in Calumet, Illinois, by the Pullman Standard Company. The wash basins were just like in a Pullman car with the little rabbit ears that stood up, you know, instead of nozzles, and all flexible couplings so the working of the ship wouldn't affect them. And the ship was built on straight British design. All the manning tables and everything else were British. It was the same as a corvette in the British Navy.

Q: How big was it?

Mr. Bond: It was 193 feet long, 900 tons, and had a ram bow. It had two 1,200-horsepower Elco diesel engines just like a switch engine. The British crew was about 65; ours was 80 plus 11 corpsmen. R was in parentheses for rescuer. It was a patrol craft escort (rescue). We had a doctor and 11 pharmacist's mates. The British had three commissioned officers and two warrant officers. We had 11 officers.

Q: It must have been awfully crowded.

Mr. Bond: It was really hard to figure out things for them to do. You know, five of the officers were assistants to five others, and the odd one was captain.* And he was odd.

Q: Why do you say that?

Mr. Bond: Well, he had no sea duty except a very short time on the battleship North Carolina when it was going

---

*The first commanding officer of the USS PCE(R)-858 was Lieutenant Franklin H. Beardsley, Jr., USNR.

through shakedown and he was a new ensign. The man with the most experience at sea officer among the officers was the supply officer, who was not in the Supply Corps. He was a line officer with supply as his billet. But he'd been captain of a subchaser in the Caribbean.

Q: Where had this captain been all during the war?

Mr. Bond: Shore assignments. In civilian life he was a history teacher, and we actually had a guy in the crew that had a class from him.

Q: Was the skipper a lieutenant?

Mr. Bond: He was a full lieutenant. And he was a nice enough fellow.

There were only 12 or 13 of us that went up to Chicago and brought the ship down the Mississippi River. We had one junior officer by the name of Foster, who was only 19 years old and just really gullible.* He was a nice kid, but we took advantage of him. We got into Chicago and were right at the Naval Reserve armory, and we said, "Now, the thing we want you to do is get us three-out-of-four liberty." He came back crestfallen; he couldn't arrange that, but he got us this every-other-day liberty starting

---

*Ensign Joe C. Foster, USNR.

at noon. That was pretty good liberty.

When we got in the Naval Reserve armory, I ran into a kid off the Saratoga that I knew pretty well because he lived up in the ship's sail locker. Some people are surprised that there would be a sail locker on the Saratoga. But the people who sewed any canvas for gun covers and all that were known as sailmakers. They also had a corollary duty that they did sew the canvas for the burials.

This guy's name was Leo Matecki, and he was a hash-mark seaman from south Chicago.* My good friend Fritz Martin Kirsch on the Saratoga was also from Chicago, so they were always talking about Chicago, and that's how I got to know Leo. Then I found him working in the scullery in the Naval Reserve armory. He had gotten transferred right after I did. Since he had five years of sea duty, serving all through the war, the Navy was just going to put him where he could get home the maximum amount of time.

Every time we took our trays through, you know, Leo would see us, and he'd yell, "V for Victory," push another tray and stuff it into the dishwasher.

Anyway, we fooled around there on Lake Michigan a little bit. We went out one time and sort of followed the

---

*Seaman First Class Leo C. Matecki, USN, who had reported to the Saratoga on 2 December 1940.

Wolverine along as plane guard.* The PCE(R) was like a toy to us, and the fellow that was handling her as acting captain was a river pilot. After about a week he was satisfied with it, so they unstepped the mast and we went down the Illinois Waterway.

Q: Was this plane guarding with just your skeleton crew?

Mr. Bond: Yes, but we were just out for a day. And there was no big problem. We could run the ship. It was very easy.

Q: Any specific memories from working with the Wolverine?

Mr. Bond: No, except that you have to see a paddle-wheel aircraft carrier to believe it. But it looked just about the same as a regular carrier. It had a flat top and qualified pilots, which was the same old deal. I don't even know if the Wolverine had a hangar deck.

Q: I don't think either of them did; the Sable was there too.

---

*The USS Wolverine (IX-64) and USS Sable (IX-81) were former commercial passenger ships converted to aircraft landing platforms. They provided student pilots the opportunity for carrier landing qualifications on Lake Michigan, an area not threatened by enemy submarines.

Mr. Bond: Right. I don't think either one did.

Anyway, we started down the Chicago River in the Illinois Waterway. And I'll tell you, in Chicago we were big stuff. We stopped in Joliet the first night, and that was sort of fun. We went into town in our undress blues. We weren't really allowed ashore. The pilot told us he couldn't give us permission, but he left and wouldn't be back until 8:00 in the morning.

So we went up town and went to a show. Afterward we got to eat. A sailor came in, a Navy guy with all sorts of ribbons. He was about half drunk and had a girlfriend with him and all. He thought he was pretty important and asked us what we were. We said, "Oh, we're Coast Guardsmen. And all we do is ferry ships down the river. And we get sea pay for it."

Oh, he was upset and he was fighting the war, and there we were, just ferrying ships down the river, getting sea pay and all.

Q: You were baiting this guy.

Mr. Bond: Yes, right. So then the next day we went down and stopped at Peoria. And, again, the pilot had someplace to go, and we went in town, and there was a bar or restaurant that was under the street. You could go down either side--and I'm sure this is so. There was some sort of war plant there in Peoria, and mostly women worked there. These gals were there having a few drinks before they went to work. We convinced them that it'd be more fun to come down to the ship, and we'd make some steak sandwiches and things. So we had about 40 of them down to the ship. I don't know; I think we really put a dent in their production that night. And, of course, 13 guys with 40 girls, there wasn't anything you could do, anyhow. But we had a little party there.

Finally we got down to the Mississippi, and we tied up somewhere around Alton. Our reputation had gotten ahead of us, and they tied us up outside about ten coal barges. It was raining and drizzling, so we didn't go ashore. The next day they put us alongside an LST and basically went all the way down the river tied to her.

Q: And the mast was restepped, I take it.

Mr. Bond: Oh, sure. The mast was restepped.

Q: I'd be interested in your recollections of working with this pilot. That's an old art, going back to Mark Twain.*

---

*Mark Twain was the pen name of noted American novelist Samuel Clemens, who had worked as a Mississippi River pilot from 1857 to 1861. The term "mark twain" meant the water was two fathoms deep when measured by leadsman casting a weighted line into the river.

Mr. Bond: You know, when you're at sea one thing you don't ever want to do is run aground--certainly not on purpose. But I remember one time when we were coming along and just sort of drifting with the current. There was a railroad bridge and this just unending train of coal cars going across. Finally, the pilot said, "Well, just run her ashore right over there. That's a nice place."

"What do you mean?"

He says, "Just nose her in. We'll wait for the train." So we waited for the train, and the train left, and we just backed off. But he said he parked there a lot of times.

Q: Did the bridge then open up?

Mr. Bond: Yes, then the bridge opened up and we went through. We were getting into Peoria towards the evening, and it was getting dark. He said, "Now, when you hear a dog barking ahead, I want you to come right, right away. Don't wait for me."

We were going along, and there was this big bluff up ahead. All of a sudden I heard a dog bark. He said, "Come right, come right!" So I came right, and the river made a right-angle turn.

I said, "What's going to happen when that dog dies?"

He said, "The next guy's going to have problems. But after that everybody will know."

He lived in this community that was maybe a couple thousand miles long and just 100 yards wider than the river. We'd pass houseboats or something, and he'd run out on the wing of the bridge and yell, "Hi, Mabel. Hello, George. Did you see Fred?"

"Yeah, I saw him two days ago." That sort of thing.

What really amazed me was how little civilization you could see from the river. Then you hit a town or a city that was on the river. But you'd go miles and miles and miles, and you could really believe that this is just the way it looked when the first guys came by, because people have stayed back from the river. One thing that was amazing was how deep the river was down by Natchez, Mississippi. As I recall, it's several hundred feet deep through that gorge there.

Q: How did you find out how deep it was--just by the charts?

Mr. Bond: No, the sonic depth finder, which was functional.

Q: You certainly couldn't use a lead line.

Mr. Bond: No, not in that deep water. But it was a lot of fun. The pilot and I did all the steering until we got tied up to the LST.

Finally we came to the end of our river trip. When we first arrived at New Orleans, we went to the Navy base at Algiers, and they put us in dry dock. Almost every ship that came down the river had damage to her screws, so they wanted to inspect that. About that time the first class electrician's mate went to the captain, and he said, "Captain, do you know that this dry dock's got a PA system?"

The captain said, "Well, I never thought about it. But I know that this ship hasn't got a PA system."

The electrician's mate said, "I know that. We don't rate it, but I could install the dry dock's PA system on the ship." So that night we removed the PA system from the dry dock and he installed it. We were the only PCE(R) with a PA system.

That was sort of the way that ship worked. Now, this was a huge change for me. You know, most of the petty officers were off of big ships. We had a gunner's mate from the Washington. And the first class signalman had served on several ships, but he was originally off the Oklahoma. And the electrician's mate was also from Oklahoma, where he'd been the bridge electrician. The guys had not seen each other since Pearl Harbor.

After the dry dock we went into a little boatyard called Bollin's Boatyard. Of course, that's when the rest of the crew joined us. When we got to Bollin's, we were right in the French Quarter. The cook just gave up serving any kind of a lunch, you know, because we'd walk across the street and had lunch over there--French dip sandwiches or something like that.

That yard did a lot of woodwork in the ship: building cabinets and chart cabinets and things of that sort in our area. They generally spruced her up, and the ship was actually commissioned there around May 5. Then we went to Key West for shakedown. That was sort of fun, because they were training submarine crews too. We'd go out and hunt them, and they'd try to evade us. And we really had a lot of antisubmarine gear because we were so British. We had the pilothouse below the open bridge, and the asdic hut was built into the forward part of the bridge.* We had good sonar gear and a Hedgehog launcher on there.** Of course, we had depth charges. We had a 3-inch gun and two single-barrel 40s. But the Hedgehogs and depth charges were our real weapons. During the shakedown we really beat the hell out of a couple of those subs with plaster-loaded Hedgehogs.

---
*Asdic was the British acronym for sonar.
**Hedgehog was the name of a British-designed mortar-type antisubmarine weapon. It was launched out ahead of the ship, rather than going off the stern as depth charges did.

Bond #2 - 222

Q: Now, the war in Europe ended during this period.*

Mr. Bond: Yes.

Q: Was it intended originally that you'd operate in the Atlantic?

Mr. Bond: Yes, that's what the intention was, and we were attached to the Atlantic Fleet.

One thing I should mention about this ship was that it was very well painted. We started out with a very peculiar light blue--not a baby blue, but something that Pullman Standard came up with. As soon as we got to New Orleans that had to be changed. We painted the ship the Atlantic colors, which basically meant the hull was pretty dark and then a lighter superstructure. Observation from a periscope would make it difficult to spot the ship on the horizon, because it would blend in.

Later we got transferred to the Pacific Fleet. The people there told us to paint on the seven-color camouflage pattern. I told the captain, "There aren't any ships out there that are painted that way. They have discontinued that."

He said, "Well, this is my directive." At the time

---

*Germany officially surrendered to the Allied Powers on 8 May 1945.

the paint was really just barely dry from painting the Atlantic colors, but he said, "We have to do it." So we progressed outward to Pearl Harbor, and we painted a camouflage job en route. When we went into Pearl, we were the only ship with camouflage that just stood out like a sore thumb. The very first message we got was to change the paint job on that ship to a dark blue that would blend in with the sea when seen from the air. So, of course, we started painting it again.

Then came a progression of the things. We went out to Okinawa in time for the end of the war, and then went up to Japan. They told us to paint it in peacetime gray, which we proceeded to do. After the war we were sort of stable for a while, paint-wise. Then we came back to the States, and we went back to Key West. They were going to put the ship in the reserve fleet, and we started painting it in preservative. Now, we didn't quite get that done before they decided they were going to turn it over to the Coast Guard. Then we took it up to Charleston and painted it white. I think that they used more paint on that little ship in less than a year--ten months from commissioning--than they did on the _Saratoga_, if you don't count the blue wash we put on the flight deck.

Anyway, getting back, then we left Key West, and we went down to Panama. We transited the canal, which I really enjoyed; it made a huge impression on me. We arrived at Colon, went into Coco Solo Navy Base, and we spent a couple of days there. Then we went up into Gatun Lake and anchored there. They were anchoring a lot of ships in Gatun Lake in those days because it was very secure. The war up in Atlantic was over, but, anyway, they were still doing it. It was a good opportunity to hose down the ship with fresh water, and we had a water fight. We divided the crew into port and starboard sections and broke out the fire hoses. Boy, that was fun. When you get hit full bore from a fire hose, it'd knock you right overboard, which wouldn't be any problem on that ship because of the low freeboard.

The next day we went through the canal, and I steered all the way. It's all done by ranges.* Those locks impressed me a lot. The Mississippi River locks did not, but those locks really impressed me. When you go into a lock, the guy threw that heaving line over to you, and then you hauled in the towing hawser. I swear those guys could throw that heaving line right through the hawsepipe if you wanted them to. They were good. Which just goes to show you if people practice enough, they get awfully good at something.

Q: Were these Panamanians?

---
*A navigational range is a pair of lights or day beacons on shore used to mark a line of bearing. When the observer on board a ship sees one of the lights or beacons directly over the other, he knows he is in the proper position.

Mr. Bond: Yes, they were civilians that worked for the canal. Most of them probably had worked there for years and years and years. I understand it was a very prized job.

Q: Well, those locks are a lot bigger than the ones on the Mississippi.

Mr. Bond: Oh, yes, that's right.

So then we escorted four LSTs 4,444 nautical miles to Pearl Harbor. We weren't long in Pearl, but I did get a chance to go over to the Saratoga. After we'd been there a couple days, they moved us down by Hospital Point. We were in the middle of a nest of ships, and guys were coming and going. All of a sudden, we just decided we were going to run a regulation ship. We had enough guys around that had been on big ships, and we had a fellow with a trumpet that knew the bugle calls. So, by God, you couldn't cross the "Be-No" without permission. And we used the bugle to call away the motor whaleboat and to sound liberty call. The captain was just absolutely mystified. He didn't know what was going on, but he sort of liked it. The enlisted men took over, and we'd do things like that.

Between the forward and after engine rooms was the chill and dry food storage space. It was below the galley, which was on the main deck. There was a ladder down to there, and the cooks would go down and pull food out. They noticed there was food disappearing, so they changed the lock on the storage room hatch. It was padlocked with a hasp and all. After that the food was still disappearing--not big amounts but especially prize leftovers. Because of the size of the ship, the officers were eating out of that galley too. Their leftovers were better than the average ones. Finally they said only the first class cook could carry the key, but the food still disappeared. The captain told the supply officer, "We changed those locks every time and food still disappeared."

This really was getting on the captain's nerves, and real overtones of Captain Queeg, even though this preceded Queeg.* It got to the point they had a combination lock on the storage room, and only the captain knew it. If the cook wanted to draw stores, the captain had to go down and open the chill box. The food still disappeared. Then they finally gave up, took the lock off, and the food quit disappearing.

Because the ship was small, it rolled easily; a motor launch would go by and it would roll. Since it might be hazardous to cart around big bottles of acetylene and

---

*Lieutenant Commander Philip F. Queeg, USN, was the fictitious commanding officer of the destroyer-minesweeper USS Caine in Herman Wouk's classic naval novel of World War II, The Caine Mutiny, published by Doubleday & Company in 1951. Queeg was a mentally unstable martinet, so his name has become associated with overbearing, eccentric skippers.

oxygen for welding jobs, the shop back aft on the main deck was equipped with really long hoses. When night would come, we would use those hoses and torches to cut the hasp off, take out what we wanted, weld the hasp back on, and repaint it. It looked just the same as before the theft. So that whole episode was just a recreational type of bedevilment for the crew.

That was the only ship I've ever heard of where men voluntarily used seniority to get on a stores working party. Our supply officer would lure the storekeeper away when the working party went to a supply depot ashore, and then the guys would just grab everything in sight. We got away with almost a whole motor whaleboat full of boned turkey. It lasted for the rest of the life of the ship.

We had three cooks in the crew. When we were getting commissioned, the third class cook came to the captain and said, "I have a confession to make."

The captain said, "What is it?"

He said, "I'm not a cook."

"What do you mean you're not a cook?"

"Well, my last ship wanted to give me a pay raise and rate me, and cook's rate was open."

The captain said, "God, what are you?"

He says, "I'm a baker."

"Don't worry, your secret is safe with me."

This kid loved to bake. You'd go to the mess there, and you might have your choice of three different kinds of bread and a choice of pie or cake for dessert, because he just baked all night long. We assigned some seaman or something to help out in the galley, so that two cooks could handle the meals.

Q: It sounds as if you had a great time on that ship.

Mr. Bond: Well, it was and it wasn't, because it wasn't the Navy, and I got awfully tired of painting. But that baking was important later on. When we got up to Okinawa, we took a couple merchantmen out to Tinian and dropped them there, and then we went up to Okinawa. It was VJ Day when we got to Okinawa.*

All of a sudden, there was this huge typhoon, and we were the smallest ship that was sent to sea.** We went out and more or less moved up to the North China Sea--away from the typhoon. I remember we followed the Coast Guard Cutter _Bibb_, and all I can remember for a couple of nights was just the stern light on the _Bibb_ and following that.

Then, instead of going back to Buckner Bay, we were

---
*VJ Day--victory over Japan, the date of the Japanese cessation of hostilities, which was 15 August 1945 in the Far East and 14 August in the United States.
**A typhoon in the Okinawa area, 16-18 September 1945, killed 89 U.S. officers and enlisted men, as well as sinking a submarine chaser and four small minesweepers. A second typhoon, on 10 October, devastated the southern end of Okinawa, leaving many persons without shelter.

detached and sent south of Kyushu to join the APA-200, the <u>Marathon</u>, which was an attack transport that had been torpedoed.* It was used to run over areas where we had sown pressure mines. The PCE(R) was going to be the APA's tender and take off her crew. The <u>Marathon</u> kept a few guys that could manage the ship from the bridge. The interesting thing about this is that when the Japanese team went down to arrange the cease-fire, they brought mine charts with them. The Japanese had heavily mined Japanese home waters. We went right through a mine field south of Kyushu. The controlling depth was something like 15 feet, and we only drew nine feet of water. Everybody was asking, "Is that nine feet from the crest or the trough?" After the storm we used rifle fire to destroy about four or five mines that we saw floating on the surface. But I'll tell you, there were really very few guys that were down below during that trip across there. To see these ugly black mines floating there really made you nervous.

Q: Did you still have your medical people on at this time?

Mr. Bond: Yes, they were still there.

---

*The USS <u>Marathon</u> (APA-200) was a 10,680-ton transport that landed troops during amphibious assaults. On 22 July 1945, while at Buckner Bay, Okinawa, she was badly damaged when hit by a kaiten suicide craft from the <u>I-53</u>. After repairs the ship returned to Okinawa in September and then was used for minesweeping from October 1945 to February 1946.

Q: What was the intended mission of the ship? I presume it was to go along with convoys.

Mr. Bond: That was the original intention. Out of every convoy there was one ship designated as a rescue ship. Somebody somewhere had arrived at the fact that it'd be better if there was a ship fitted for rescue work. So they were going to make up these convoy groups and these PCEs or corvettes, and one of them would be a rescue ship. To make room for the medical space, our boat deck was extended farther aft in a rather ungainly profile with a little back porch for the fantail. Then they had X-ray equipment and operating room and that sort of thing.

Q: When the war ended, though, that mission went away.

Mr. Bond: That's right. So then we had a nice big passenger compartment. It was really pretty good, because we could knock those bunks down, and we had a fairly open compartment there. But that made an ideal ship to take the crew off the _Marathon_ and put them up. So then we followed the _Marathon_ around. The _Marathon_ never did detonate a pressure mine. They went all over this place. Of course, these B-29 pilots and their crews that had dropped these things, you can imagine how precise their location was.*

---

*The B-29 was a U.S. Army Air Forces heavy bomber that was also used for dropping atomic bombs on Hiroshima, Japan, on 6 August 1945 and on Nagasaki, Japan, on 9 August.

Q: Not very.

Mr. Bond: Not even flying low over the Inland Sea. The only amazing thing was that the U.S. forces basically occupied Japan by the same format as the invasion would have been. The same people went to those places, and a lot of British came in there at Kure. A lot of transports came in Kure: ships coming and going, and personnel; literally thousands of men disembarked. All that was over; all the ships had gone; a sleepy little thing of an LST was coming up the bay one day and Bam! There went one of these pressure mines. They were supposed to deactivate themselves in a certain period of time, but you had to be sure.

Well, anyway, after we went with the Marathon quite a bit, then we were assigned as a command ship to minesweepers to sweep the conventional mines and we did that because we had the sick bay. They anchored every night. Every morning their men on sick call would come over to spend the day aboard us while the rest of the crew went out and swept. Then when they finished that area, we'd move up the coast a little bit. It was sort of interesting.

Q: You didn't really cover specifically the end of the

war. How did you find out that news, and what was the reaction on board ship?

Mr. Bond: Oh, my. Well, the reaction aboard ship and all the other ships was jubilation. When we were in Buckner Bay thousands of guys were on the beach, guns going off, ships' whistles and sirens, and all sorts of things-- anything anybody could do to celebrate. They just tried to be restrained to the extent that things wouldn't get out of control. But it was pretty hard to restrain it. I understand even back at Pearl they were firing guns in the air a little bit.

Q: Did you feel a sense of relief that you'd made it?

Mr. Bond: Yes, and almost disbelief. It's like being on a long, long hike, and you've gotten to the point where you just keep going. Then all of a sudden somebody said, "We're here."

Q: Well, the end came sooner than expected.

Mr. Bond: Yes, that's right.

You say, "Is this it? We really are here?" You thought the end of the hike was still miles on. Of course, we'd heard about the two bombs and all that, and we were up there in Kure with the <u>Marathon</u> before really anybody else was there. A few guys were beginning to make arrangements, and they offered to take a bunch of us over to Hiroshima in their truck. And that, I'm telling you, was an astounding sight. Now, Kure was just as flat as Hiroshima, but that had been done by high explosive and incendiaries from many, many bombers and, of course, it was the major naval construction base. That was where some of the biggest Japanese ships were built in graving docks.

Q: Did you have an emotional reaction to what you saw at Hiroshima?

Mr. Bond: Oh, yes. Now, we had gotten our cameras back. The captain released them. The guys had quite a bit of film aboard ship, but we didn't have any way to develop it. One of the motor machinist's mates, a fellow named Todd, was quite a chemist.* He decided that X-ray developer solution would work on regular film if it was weakened down. He got it to work. Then there were fellows that had done a little photographic printing, and they rigged up a way to make contact prints. So then the captain tried to get some photographic paper through channels. No way. I was part of a delegation that went over to a command ship there in Buckner Bay and went down to the photographer's

---

*Motor Machinist's Mate First Class Merritt H. Todd, USN.

shop. Our guys asked all these questions about printing photos. And the photographers asked, "What ship you off?"

I told them the number of our ship, and I said, "Well, one of the great things is the food on the ship. We have an excellent baker and we get homemade pies."

The guy said, "You do?"

"Yeah."

"Boy, that'd be good to have."

"Well, I'll tell you. If you can fix us up with some photographic paper, we'll fix you up with some pies and cakes." So we did, and they did. That just shows you that unofficial channels work better than official when you didn't have any real reason to have this stuff. But, anyway, any pictures that anybody took, they made prints for the whole crew. You'd come to breakfast in the morning, and one mess table would be full of prints. You just took what you wanted. We took a lot of pictures of Hiroshima, including the classic one of that building surrounded by rubble.

Q: But you were, I guess, stunned just to see the devastation that had been inflicted.

Mr. Bond: That's right. I sent those pictures back to Marilyn right away. The ones that I have are the ones I sent her. The notations that are written on the back of them were made at that time, without benefit of any later thoughts. And the thing I wrote on the back of one of the Hiroshima pictures was, "Just imagine, this is one bomb, and a small one at that." That gives you a fair idea of what that impression was.

Q: Did you encounter any Japanese people?

Mr. Bond: Yes, and I would say at that time you could have closed your eyes and walked down a crowded sidewalk and you'd never hit anybody. They'd have jumped in the gutter up to their knees. They were very frightened of us. Every time you went by, the police bowed and saluted and drew their swords, that sort of thing. The Japanese were so shocked, I guess, at this that there was no bitterness. The cleavage was complete--one day and it was a new world.

Q: The Emperor told them, "It's over."

Mr. Bond: Yes, and the knowledge of Hiroshima and Nagasaki was general. I mean, the people understood--especially the people where we were.

One night when we were with the minesweepers, we were in a little town in the harbor on the Shikoku side. We found out it was a fishing preserve. We fished off the ship, and we filled two or three milk cans with fish in about half an hour and sold them to the Japanese. Then we started doing that regularly because the minesweepers were out; all we had to do was kill time all day. So we had a whole dishpan full of Japanese money. When you went ashore on liberty and thought you needed money, you just grabbed a handful out of that before you went.

We did get to several different places around the Inland Sea and saw quite bit of that. It's a very beautiful area.

Then, at this time, I got some mail from Marilyn, my present wife. Several weeks earlier, before we got to Okinawa, there was mail waiting for us at Tinian. Marilyn was at USC at this time. In her letters she was telling me about all the parties and all the servicemen that were back there in school. It just sort of made me angry, so I sat down and wrote her a letter and just told her off. I mailed the letter in Okinawa. When we were out in that storm, the LST that was the mail post office went aground and a lot of mail got lost and strayed. We didn't get any mail for a while. I was sort of ticked, and I decided I was going to just stay in the Navy.

By the time we got to Shikoku, Grant Mainland, who had been supply officer had moved up to become the exec.* On a ship that small, that meant he was the navigator, so he and I worked together closely. He had gone to the University of California at Berkeley through the ROTC program. Then he had, as I said, had command of that

---

*Lieutenant David G. Mainland, USNR; exec--executive officer.

subchaser. I liked Grant pretty well, and I was sort of tending towards either USC or Berkeley. If it hadn't been for the GI Bill, Berkeley being a state college or state university, it'd been more possible financially.* Anyway, he knew about me telling off Marilyn.

Finally we got some mail, and I had three letters. I arranged them chronologically. The first one just refuted everything I said and more or less wondered whether I was just paranoid or something more serious. Then the next two went on as if nothing had happened. I was sitting up on the ready box on the signal bridge while I was reading them. Grant came up and said, "Letters from Marilyn?"

I said, "Yes."

"Guess you're going to reconsider staying in the Navy."

I said, "Yeah, I think so." But, anyway, that was sort of a humorous event. This was in November or early December because it was pretty darn cold. Then we were sent back to the States. We left behind all the men with quite a bit of time to do, and we filled in some bunks and billets with guys whose time was up or had enough points to go back to the States. I'd say we wandered back to the States all by ourselves. The ship went to Eniwetok and then to Pearl and on to San Diego.

---

*The GI Bill, officially the Servicemen's Readjustment Act of 1944, provided educational assistance and other benefits to all veterans honorably discharged with six or more months of active service after 16 September 1940.

Q: You probably would have had enough points to get out had you not been regular Navy.*

Mr. Bond: Yes, about this time I would have. But, still it wasn't too bad. A lot of guys were leaving. When we left Japan, each of us was given a Japanese rifle, which I still have.

We didn't stay at Pearl long at all, just a couple of days. When we got back to San Diego, we were tied up right down by the city hall there, and that baker of ours only lived two blocks away. He was Italian, and I guess that his relatives filled up just about whole block. They just had a 24-hour party for us, for anybody who could come by-- tables of food. We had a good time. We stayed in San Diego about a week and then went down the coast to Panama, and through the canal again. We got into Colon Harbor after dark. I was on the wheel, and I was really tired. It'd been a long day. The last time, you remember, we had stopped in Gatun Lake and then gone from the lake the next day. This time we went all the way through the same day. I steered that whole way, for ten hours.

There we were, wandering around Colon Harbor, when we were supposed to go to Coco Solo. And the water tower at

---

*For the demobilization of the U.S. armed forces after World War II, the services had a point system to determine individual priorities for leaving the service. Points were awarded for length of service, overseas service, battle stars, decorations, and dependent children. Those with the highest number of points were the earliest discharged.

Coco Solo had a signal tower above it. I was reading the light there. Anybody could tell that it was the signal tower with the blinking light. Certainly the captain should have known. By now this was Lieutenant Black, who had been first lieutenant and was now captain of the ship.* I just really forgot that I was standing in front of a voice tube that went up to the open bridge. I turned to lee helmsman and said, "You know, the captain couldn't even get a driver's license, much less conn this ship." But it just went out over the open bridge, and then I heard the voice of the officer of the deck, charged with emotion, say, "Bond, go below."

"Aye, aye, sir." After all that time on the bridge, I was tired, and I did get relieved, but I was really in the doghouse. So the rest of my time aboard I had sort of a difficult relationship with the captain.

So then we went up to Key West, and we were getting the ship ready to go up the St. John's River at Jacksonville. Key West was sort of interesting then. They had some German pocket submarines and German naval personnel there, just fooling around with them. There were a couple of other captured subs and sub crews, and the U.S. Navy was sort of trying them out to see what was new.

But the main thing that made it so much fun was that

---

*Lieutenant William H. Black, USNR.

we were tied up right by the WAVES barracks.* The WAVES were really hard to get acquainted with, but we had quite a few Californians, and in those days barbecuing wasn't the nationwide pastime it is now. In our free and easy situation it seemed like as the crew got smaller and smaller, the amount of the food didn't change. So we were really living high off the hog. We decided that in trying to chase the WAVES, the thing we'd do was have the WAVES chase us. So we went over to the beach and built a barbecue, and we had a big beach barbecue, and invited the WAVES. Now, we only invited ten or something. We could only accommodate ten, see, and this created the demand, a scarcity. So we had a lot of parties with the WAVES and got acquainted with them. Then the ship sent a leave party off. By now the crew was down to about 40 guys or something like that. When the leave party was gone, it left about 20.

Then we got orders to go up to Charleston. We were missing a lot of rates because when they made up the leave party, nobody gave any thought to divisions or sections or watches because the ship wasn't expected to move. But now we didn't have any radiomen or we didn't have a radarman. So we borrowed some guys from the receiving station and headed up to Charleston. We arrived there on a very, very

---

*WAVES was the acronym for Women Accepted for Volunteer Emergency Service. Years later, after the women were incorporated into the regular Navy, the term WAVES was no longer used.

foggy day, and nothing was working. We couldn't make radio contact with the beach. The radar was out of kilter. The topography of the area was such that there weren't any great features--the lighthouse being the most prominent one, and that was changing bearing all the time on this radar. We found one buoy, but we couldn't pick up the sea buoy.

So we got close and anchored and tried to put a boat in the water. And the davits wouldn't work; they were frozen or rusted. Then we got the other one in the water and found out we couldn't start the boat. But we could start the boat that was up on the blocks on the other davit, so we rigged a boom and lowered the boat. And, you know, we're talking about a couple hours of effort, and we finally got over to the buoy. We found out it was a dredging company's buoy and not on a chart or anything like that. About that time the bell cracked. Of course, in the fog we were ringing the bell every minute.

As I mentioned, I hadn't been getting along with Captain Black since Coco Solo. Then, all of a sudden, just when it looked like he was really going to get angry, he burst out laughing. He sat down and just laughed and laughed. It was just unbelievable, everything. Shortly after that, somebody just looking in the radio shack noticed this switch that had voice and audio, and said, "What's this?" and flipped it to voice. We could communicate with the beach, and they gave us a bearing for the sea buoy. We picked it up and came right in.

After we got settled there, as I said, we started painting the ship white and surveying everything. The crew dwindled down, and finally the last few of us turned it over to the Coast Guard.

Q: Did you have a formal decommissioning ceremony?

Mr. Bond: Not really.

The main thing I got out of my service in the "Be-No," the thing I really enjoyed, was that I navigated the ship from Japan to Key West. Grant Mainland let me do it, and he had confidence in me. He didn't like getting up early to shoot stars, and I really enjoyed that. That was sort of a rare privilege.

Now that the war was over, people talked about going back to their civilian jobs. And there were guys who had some pretty good jobs. One day I said, "Mr. Mainland, what are you going back to?"

He was from the San Francisco Bay area, and he said, "Well, I guess I'm going back to the recreation department of the city of Piedmont."

I said, "What do you mean?"

He said, "Well, that's the job I had when I went in the Navy, as playground director. Gee, I sure hope I get back in time to get an A playground instead of a B."

I said, "What's the difference?"

"If it rains, you get paid if you're on an A rather than a B."

Jumping ahead several years, in 1957 our family moved to the bay area, and I looked up Grant Mainland. Believe it or not, he was the recreational director of the city of Alameda. He actually had gone back to recreation. And, of course, this was a very good job for him, because it also included physical education in the Alameda schools, which was a unique thing. So we had some good times together. In fact, we used the company tickets to Candlestick Park a number of times.*

Q: So I guess he got an A playground.

Mr. Bond: He got an A playground. He had the thrill of having my son work for him one summer as playground director. He called me up and said, "This is a very sobering experience, having a second generation."

But, anyway, when we decommissioned the PCE(R), my time was just about up, and they ordered me to Terminal Island, California, at San Pedro. I had separate orders; I wasn't in the draft at all. They gave me a train ticket and $11.05 expense money. There was one jarring note: I had made myself a large seabag, guys call it a 20-year bag. I had all my stuff in there. I had also surveyed some of

---

*Candlestick Park is the stadium in which the San Francisco Giants baseball team and San Francisco 49ers football team play their home games.

the coast pilots and sailing directions into my seabag.* It was waiting to be shipped back by Railway Express, and somebody stole it. I lost all my uniforms. The only uniforms I had were the dress uniform I was in and, oddly enough, a couple of jumpers at home.

Anyhow, I took the train, but I couldn't figure out what this five cents was for, $11.05, because there was an arrangement made with the Pullman company for the meals; servicemen could eat for a dollar. And I thought, "Well, maybe it's to change trains and depots in New Orleans. But, no, they gave me a chit for that, and it was part of the through ticket." And my ticket was not only to L.A. but the Pacific Electric Railway down to San Pedro. I thought, "Well, maybe it's for that." No, they gave me another chit. Cabs were there. Finally I got down to San Pedro and went down to take the ferry over to Terminal Island, and they said, "Five cents, please." That was the end.

Q: Well, you got home after taking the ferry. Was this before your 21st birthday?

Mr. Bond: Yes. Got out June 18, the day before my birthday.

---

*In this sense, the term "survey" refers to a Navy procedure by which accountable material is expended from the records. In this case, the material was declared excess to government needs, and Bond took possession of them rather than throwing them away.

Going way back, you remember that schooner I worked on and the fellow that went into the Coast Guard with it as skipper. He was back, and I asked him if he knew of any jobs around yachts, and he did. That summer, before going back to school at USC, I worked on the yacht Valeehi, which was a 70-foot ketch that was owned by Dana Andrews.* That was sort of a fun summer. At the end of the summer Marilyn and I got married, and I went back to school as a married GI veteran.

Q: How much of your education was paid for? All tuition, what else?

Mr. Bond: It was $500.00 a year, but you see, the way it worked was if you ran over that, you had an option of paying or taking off your eligibility. Like a lot of things, it didn't work out quite the way Congress said. They set it up so that the maximum eligibility was four years, and that was then interpreted as 48 months. Then the state of California had a one-year program. So you really, essentially, had 60 months of schooling, and since you only use nine months in a school year, you had plenty of eligibility. So it covered my school tuition and books completely, because I had eligibility to burn. So I went a

---

*Dana Andrews was a leading man in movies of the era.

little bit over $500.00 a year. I was living at home so I didn't need dormitory space or anything like that. I liked the GI bill.

Q: How did you decide what to major in when you were there?

Mr. Bond: Well, I decided I was going to major in foreign trade. I really sort of discovered this major from a bulletin I had from the University of California; they also had the same major. I was still going back to my interest in the merchant marine. USC had a trade and transportation department, so I majored in foreign trade, which also had a lot of other basic transportation and business courses in the school, what's now business administration.

I went to school through the summers, too, because I wasn't interested in dragging this thing out. I knew my old age was approaching, now that I was 21 and had been passed by as the lost generation and all that. I needed a part-time job, so I got one with a little freight-forwarding company, which was a company that accumulated small shipments and loaded boxcars to Portland and Seattle. It was a pretty good job. I put the rates and charges on the bills so the girls could type them up.

The railroads were so slow that you had plenty of time to do that and mail them up to the other end, so it was very flexible. I was able to do a lot of it on Saturdays. I could really get a lot of hours in and if I had a test, I didn't have to work the night before.

I graduated in 1949 summer school, and wages were low. I couldn't find a full-time job that paid as well as my part-time job. I went down to Matson Steamship Company, and a fellow there really wanted me to work for him. He was going to figure out how I could get paid overtime without having to work it and all that. And I said, "How much does all this come to?"

He said, "Well, with all this it'll come to darn near $200.00 a month."

I said, "Well, I'm making $250.00 a month in a part-time job."

He said, "Well, I'd hang onto that if I were you."

So I'd go to foreign trade companies, and they'd say, "Well, you know, before the war, we'd hire somebody for this job just for the experience."

I said, "Well, I need more than that."

They said, "I know, but we certainly can't pay enough for anybody to live on."

I finally decided I was going to have to forgo that field. I'd taken an awful lot of Spanish, and I was fairly fluent in it. But being fluent in Spanish and bilingual Spanish-English in Los Angeles is no big deal. They've got a million people there that are bilingual in Spanish.

Since I really didn't have anything full time, I thought, "Well, I'll just turn to transportation." So I went to another company, a truck line called Los Angeles-Seattle Motor Express, and began working for them in 1950. That's the company I worked for until they got involved in a merger January 1, 1970. Then I came here.

Q: What sorts of jobs essentially did you do during those 20 years?

Mr. Bond: Well, the old guy that really ran L.A.-Seattle was a fellow by the name of Oscar Hendricks in Seattle. When I say "old," he was probably 40 or 42 at the time, He had taken a liking to me, and he wanted to know if I was really serious in the field; if so, he'd move me around to various things. So I worked in operations; he had me in sales for a couple of years, and I was the assistant operations manager, which meant really running the night shift in the terminal at L.A. That was a pretty good size operation; they handled over 1,000 shipments a night there, about 20 loads.

This was a very quality company, high-performance operation, and a very stable company. If I had gone back to Los Angeles, we'll say, in '69 before the merger, virtually all the people that I knew in 1950 were still there. There had been a few added, but the ones who were there hadn't left. This included drivers and dock men, dispatchers and all. It was really a tight-knit thing. We had an excellent operation because we all were in a parallel path. We worked together naturally, and we had the same objectives and standards. But if you were chafing for advancement, that wasn't the place to be.

In '57 they were planning on building a new terminal in the San Francisco Bay area. We had a small terminal on both sides of the Bay--San Francisco and Oakland--and this was awkward. Of course, these things are all tradeoffs, but they decided that it would be better to build a major terminal on the Oakland side. So the fellow who was district manager asked me if I wanted to be the district traffic manager for the area, and I said, "Sure." Because I really did want to move out of Los Angeles.

Q: Why was that?

Mr. Bond: Well, it was just getting so crowded. We'd moved down by Santa Monica Bay, a place called Playa Del Rey. It's before they had Marina Del Rey. But this is an area just west of the airport. It was just a little enclave down there, about three streets deep and a mile or so long, and it was right on the beach and we really enjoyed it.

I got involved with a neighbor who wanted to start a

Boy Scout troop. We'd take the kids on weekend overnight campouts. When I saw how far we had to go to get to a place where the kids would consider themselves out on the trip, rather than just camping in the park, it just really brought home to me how sprawling and big that city was. I'd been a Boy Scout in Los Angeles when I was young. I remembered one place we went to before, and I told the kids it was really a good place where you could hike. One group could hike in from the valley side and one from the city side, and meet in this place.

We thought we'd do that and stash food, and then the first group would go out to the second group's starting point and vice-versa and pick up the food on the way. The key to it was, of course, that you get to someplace that's sort of special and you can't drive to. Then we came into this place, a little valley I remembered as being isolated. There was a road in there, and there were hundreds of people there. The kids said, "What's so hot about this, and why did we walk over a mountain to get to it?" I was really sort of fed up with the pressure and the population, and the smog was getting bad.

Q: Had you given any consideration to the Naval Reserve during that period after the war?

Mr. Bond: Well, only in a monetary way when things were sort of tight and my salary was low. A friend of mine joined the Naval Reserve and suggested I join because I was discharged as a second class pretty officer. By the way, as soon as I went to PCE(R), I was rated second class because they had an opening. After he saw my examination results, the executive officer said, "Well, I'm certainly not going to argue with qualifications of the Saratoga. I'll take their word for it."* So I made my rate very easily after commissioning.

Unfortunately, the reserve unit my friend was in didn't have any quartermasters, so obviously I couldn't enlist in grade there. They told me there was a unit down at Long Beach, or San Pedro or something, that did have quartermasters. But I never got around to going down there, and it was just 50 miles away. Then, shortly after that, the Korean War broke out, and quartermaster was one rate they called pretty universally. At that time, with a wife and a couple of little kids, I would not have wanted to go back in the service. So I never did get around to joining the reserve.

I wasn't interested in any veterans' organizations either. Somebody tried to start an American Legion post for men that had served on the Saratoga. They had a couple

---

*The first executive officer of the PCE(R)-858 was Lieutenant Maurice J. Petrosky, USNR.

meetings, and I went to one of them. Most of the guys I didn't even know. The only thing that was really interesting was that there was an old fellow there that was a veteran of the previous Saratoga.

Q: She had originally been the New York. Then she got renamed the Saratoga and still later the Rochester.*

Mr. Bond: But that was sort of a kick, to have somebody from a different Saratoga than we were talking about. But it had lacked any cohesiveness, and even though there were enough guys around the L.A. area to have a group, they were spread all over the place and for a special event, they all wanted to see if they could find somebody they knew. They'd come together. But that was the nearest I ever came to getting into a veterans' organization.

Q: In the late '50s, you moved up to San Francisco.

Mr. Bond: About that time, they redesigned and restructured the airport in Los Angeles and moved the runway from where it was, taking off over a vacant area, to

---

*The USS New York was armored cruiser number 2. She was commissioned 1 August 1893 and served in the Spanish-American War. On 16 February 1911 she was renamed Saratoga so that a new battleship could be the New York, and on 1 December 1917 was renamed Rochester so a new battle cruiser could be the Saratoga. Instead, the battle cruiser was converted to the aircraft carrier in which Bond served.

an area farther north. You'd almost think they used my chimney as a sighting line for the new one. And I knew they were doing that.

Then I was up in Seattle and stood down at the end of the runway at Boeing Field. A friend of mine took me down, and I saw a 707 they were testing. It took off over us, and knowing that Los Angeles was building a runway and hearing that 707, I thought to myself, "I have got to move before this happens." And so I did. Now, interestingly enough, the airport finally had to buy out all those houses and raze them, and it's all just sand dunes again.

But I enjoyed the bay area. There's a lot less population pressure. It's a more temperate climate, more what I like, more trees. I was still with the same company so I had a feeling that it was like being in the service, just changing ships, very similar to that. So I just stayed with it, and I kept telling myself, "I'll end up in Seattle one of these days." I really like Seattle. That'd be the only place that I'd contemplate moving to.

Q: That was the head office.

Mr. Bond: Yes, that was the head office. I wouldn't move today because the kids are now living here. But Seattle would be one place I would consider because Seattle is one of the best water resources around. The chief signalman on the *Saratoga* and another chief owned a sailboat on Puget Sound. Before the war they'd spend their leaves on it. One would take the month of July and the other the month of August or something. He told me that the only time they ever visited the same place twice was when they really wanted to go back. They never had to go to the same place. There's a variety of islands and places there. I just love the Puget Sound.

If I'd gone up there, I had already decided I was going to live on Bainbridge Island. That is a terrific place. In fact, that was at one time reserved for the Navy. The trees are so tall and true and all, they were set aside for Navy masts. Of course, with the passing of the need for wooden masts, they released it. But it still has beautiful tall trees, and they hadn't got cut over. But I've been very happy and satisfied in the Twin Cities.

Q: How did that come about? You said your company was reorganized in '69?

Mr. Bond: Yes, three companies merged together. The surviving management was the one that was in Lubbock, Texas, so the main office was in Lubbock. Somebody said, "You know, if you play your cards right, you could end up in the general office."

I thought, "Gosh, if the best thing possible is Lubbock, Texas, I think I'd like to look elsewhere." I don't mean to run down Lubbock, but I have been there, and it really is not my type of territory. My type of territory has a lot of water and trees. Our operation was included in that merger only so the holding company that owned us entirely could control the merged company. We really didn't fit in with the other two carriers, and they had a lot of disdain for our operation. I just knew it wasn't going to last long. And it didn't.

At that time there was a strike, but I saw an ad in the paper, a trucking company advertising for a dispatcher. I wasn't interested in being a dispatcher, but it was a different company. I thought, "Well, maybe they're expanding in this area and maybe the West Coast, and they could use somebody in another capacity that was familiar with it."

So I wrote a letter to this company in St. Paul and was given the name of the man to write to. I got a telephone call back from this man. He said, "Obviously, you're not applying for the dispatcher job, but how would you feel about living in St. Paul or Minneapolis?"

I said, "Well, I have nothing against that."

He said, "Well, we're coming out to interview the applicants for the dispatcher job, and I'd like to talk to you." So we got together, and we hit it off very well. He went back and told the president, I guess, that I'd be worth talking to. So they flew me here for an interview. The following week, he called and offered me the job and said, "How much time would your present company want as notice?"

I said, "Since they're now closed down by a strike, I wouldn't be surprised if they were pretty liberal."

So sure enough, they said, "Heck, if you want to go in a week, that's okay." So one week later, I was here.

Q: What was the name of the company you joined?

Mr. Bond: It was E. L. Murphy Trucking Company, a heavy machinery carrier, which was pretty interesting. It was a lot different from what I had been doing in many ways, but similar in other ways--still transportation.

I worked for E. L. Murphy for about five years, and then the man that had been my contact left and became president of a company that was a subsidiary of a produce brokerage company. He talked me into coming over there. We worked together there for ten years. And then with deregulation of the trucking industry and a lot of other things, the company wasn't going too well. The management of the parent company decided to sell the truck line. So this fellow and I started our own truck line. Well, it's his ownership, and he and I started it up and that's the little company we have going now.

Q: What's the name of that one?

Mr. Bond: It's Wise Way Motor Freight. His name is Hal Wiseman. We've been good friends all this time, and it's worked out pretty well.

Q: Could you just give a brief description of what the company does and how large it is?

Mr. Bond: Well, Wise Way primarily brings commercial shipments of new furniture from plants that manufacture it in Virginia, North Carolina, and Tennessee, up to Minnesota. Then we distribute throughout Minnesota and North Dakota, and South Dakota. This is not a really large market, but it's a troublesome market, especially out in the Dakotas. So we had very good reception from the plants; however, the dealers pay the freight, and ultimately control which carrier they use. But then we haul almost anything south-bound. Recently we have merged with another little carrier who had a lot of traffic south-bound but was very short of north-bound traffic. So we just fit together very well. It's about a 60-truck operation. We have about 60 tractors and 100 trailers. But I think that we've built a good reputation and have a large following through this north Midwest.

Q: Well, I know you're very proud of your family, so I think it would be appropriate to wind up this tale by discussing them.

Mr. Bond: Well, my oldest son Hal is 39 years old and lives in Portland, Oregon. After a varied career that included professional baseball and college at the University of California at Berkeley, he's a sculptor in glass, stained-glass artist. And his oldest sister is Charlene, who is 38--just 14 months younger. She is a microbiologist working at the University of Minnesota. She's married to Ted Peterson, who is a dentist here in the Twin Cities. They have no children. Our youngest daughter, Karen, who is ten years younger than Charlene, is married and lives here. She has two children: a boy now about six, seven named Jeffrey, and a little girl named Kelly. And that pretty much comprises our family.

Q: And you're still married to the woman you surprised when you were on leave back in the 1940s, so that's obviously fared well.

Mr. Bond: Yes, that's right. And, of course, you've got to remember Marilyn and I knew each other quite a while before then. We had sort of drifted away, fallen away. That happenstance of my surprise visit merely got us going again. But I think it helps that we had known each other very well, and so the adjustments were pretty easy to make.

Q: Well, you have portrayed in these last couple of days a life that includes a career as a successful businessman and a successful family man. Where does the Navy experience fit in the whole perspective?

Mr. Bond: Well, I haven't thought of that particularly. I guess the Navy experience was really a great educational experience to me, great as a person and maturing. It expanded my horizons. It gave me, I'm sure, an international viewpoint. It led me into a course of study that was certainly internationally oriented, and it gave me a firsthand appreciation for some very different parts of the world. It taught me a lot about human nature. I think in my particular business, having to deal a lot with truck drivers and dock men and things like that, it taught me how to deal with men. I think I learned a lot about leadership, and leading by example. I've seen a lot of good leaders and a lot of weak leaders. So I think that's one of the areas that my naval experience has helped me out in. And it was a natural progression, I felt, for me.

Q: Each generation gets called upon to make its particular contribution to the nation, and for your time and your place, that was World War II, and you did your job.

Mr. Bond: Yes, that's right. That's why I was not interested at that time in going into the merchant marine. The merchant marine was necessary, but I saw the need to serve in a more direct manner. I suppose a lot of it was because as a paper boy, I'd been reading and following the war, and I really identified the fact that that was a necessary job to do, was to win that war.

Q: You made that contribution then, and you've made a valuable contribution in the form of this oral history to document your service. I really appreciate that. Thank you very much.

Mr. Bond: Thank you.

Index

to

The Reminiscences of

Roger L. Bond

Advancement of Enlisted Personnel
Movie star Victor Mature moved up rapidly as an enlisted man in the Coast Guard in World War II, 141-142; advancement procedures for petty officers on board the aircraft carrier Saratoga (CV-3) in World War II, 180-182

Aircraft Carriers
A magazine article published around 1939-40 credited the Japanese with having the second-best aircraft carrier pilots in the world, 21-22; because of her characteristics, the Saratoga was not a good match for operations with the newer carriers in 1945, 198-199

Alcohol
In Hawaii during World War II, servicemen didn't have to provide proof of age in order to be able to drink, 55; the aircraft carrier Saratoga (CV-3) issued beer to crew members during port visits in World War II, 76, 78; two commanding officers of the aircraft carrier Saratoga (CV-3) took different approaches when handing out punishment for drinking-related offenses in World War II, 101-102; cheap drinks available when the Saratoga visited Hobart, Tasmania, in early 1944, 139; the British were generous with their beer allotment when operating a fleet out of Ceylon in early 1944, 150-151; drinking on board the Saratoga during World War II, 169-171; in 1944 one crew member of the British battleship Valiant had a considerable capacity for beer, 173-174

American Legion
In the years after World War II the legion had a post in California for men who had served in the crew of the aircraft carrier Saratoga (CV-3), 251-252

Antisubmarine Warfare
The destroyer Saufley (DD-465) made one unsuccessful antisubmarine attack while operating in the Solomons in late 1942, 62; shakedown training for the patrol craft PCE(R)-858 in the summer of 1945, 221-222

Atomic Bombs
See Nuclear Weapons

Australia
In early 1944 a mail clerk from the aircraft carrier Saratoga (CV-3) spent considerable time in this country while trying to get back to his ship, 111-112; liberty opportunities for American sailors in the country in World War II, 177-179

See also Australian Navy, Tasmania

Australian Navy
Supplied communications personnel for liaison duty on board the aircraft carrier Saratoga (CV-3) during her operations with the British Far Eastern Fleet in the Indian Ocean in early 1944, 145-146, 177; also provided warships for operation with the British, 148

Baltimore, USS (CA-68)
Almost became a victim of U.S. gunfire during the Gilbert Islands invasion in November 1943, 131-132

Baseball
Hall of fame player Ty Cobb went unrecognized during an airplane flight in 1944, 189-190

Beardsley, Lieutenant Franklin H., Jr., USNR
Inexperienced reserve officer who became the first skipper when the patrol craft PCE(R)-858 went into commission in the spring of 1945, 212-213, 220, 222-223, 225-227, 233

Beebe, Lieutenant Commander Robert P., USN (USNA, 1931)
As the navigator of the aircraft carrier Saratoga (CV-3), gave Bond a job interview for quartermaster in 1943, 15, 65-66; didn't evince much interest in flying, 66-67; work with the Saratoga's quartermasters, 68, 70-71; involved in advancement of petty officers, 180-181

Black, Lieutenant William H., USNR
Reserve officer who commanded the patrol craft PCE(R)-858 briefly following the end of World War II, 238-239, 241

Blanchard, Chief Electrician's Mate Frederic L., USN
Having joined the crew of the aircraft carrier Saratoga (CV-3) upon commissioning in 1927, he was still on board during World War II, 141-144

Bogan, Captain Gerald F., USN (USNA, 1916)
As commanding officer of the aircraft carrier Saratoga (CV-3) in 1942-43, was tough on men who committed drinking-related offenses, 101-102; advanced a Saratoga gunner's mate to chief petty officer after the man had knocked out Bogan in a fight, 102-103

Bond, Roger Lamar
Boyhood in Wisconsin and California in the 1920s and 1930s, 1, 10-12, 17-18, 21-22; parents of, 1, 5, 11-13, 20, 23-25; experience in the Sea Scouts in southern California in the early 1940s, 4-5, 9-10, 21, 32-33; as a public school student in the 1930s and 1940s, 14-15,

29-30; Navy enlistment and recruit training in 1942, 23-26, 28-40; as a student at the University of Southern California after World War II, 26-27, 237, 245-246; temporary duty in 1942 at the San Diego destroyer base, 41-42; wife of, 45-46, 134-135, 150, 234, 236-237, 245, 251, 258-259; service in the destroyer Saufley (DD-465) in 1942-43, 49-62; children of, 54, 243, 251, 253, 258-259; contracted a case of pneumonia while in the South Pacific in the spring of 1943, 62-64; served in the aircraft carrier Saratoga (CV-3), 1943-45, 64-206; training in Miami, Florida, 209-211; service in the patrol craft PCE(R)-858 in 1945-46, 211-243; discharge from the Navy in the spring of 1946, 243-244; postwar civilian career in the transportation business, 246-258

Brandt, Quartermaster Third Class Wilbert Hugo, USN
Passed advancement exam for second class on board the aircraft carrier Saratoga (CV-3) in 1945, 181-182

Bremerton, Washington
Liberty attractions for sailors in 1944, 192-194

See also Puget Sound Navy Yard

Breton, USS (CVE-23)
Small escort aircraft carrier that operated with a task force around the Solomon Islands in 1943, 96-97

British Far Eastern Fleet
Operations of the British in the Indian Ocean in early 1944, 125, 145-164; operations in the Dutch East Indies in 1944, 165-166, 171-173

Burial at Sea
Mass service held on board the aircraft carrier Saratoga (CV-3) for those killed by kamikazes in February 1945, 203-204

Caldwell, Commander Henry H., USN (USNA, 1927)
As air group commander in the aircraft carrier Saratoga (CV-3), suffered considerable damage to his plane while leading a strike against Rabaul, New Britain, in November 1943, 117-118; became the ship's air officer in late 1943, 166

Camouflage
The patrol craft PCE(R)-858 was repainted frequently in 1945-46 to comply with various camouflage schemes, 222-223

Cannon, Ensign Joe, USNR
    Officer who demonstrated his inexperience while on board the aircraft carrier Saratoga (CV-3) during World War II, 105-106

Cassady, Vice Admiral John H., USN (USNA, 1919)
    Conned the aircraft carrier Saratoga (CV-3) while serving as her commanding officer in 1943-44, 113-114, 124-125, 127-129, 151-152, 163-164; qualities of leadership, 121-123, 128-130, 133, 201; visited heavily damaged Eniwetok in early 1944, 138

Ceylon
    Trincomalee served as a base for the aircraft carrier Saratoga (CV-3) when she was operating with the British Far Eastern Fleet in early 1944, 125, 146, 150-151, 157, 173-174; liberty opportunities in Colombo in 1944, 155-158; Ceylonese dislike for English and Americans, 156-158

Chaplains
    Role of Lieutenant Commander Ozias B. Cook as ship's chaplain in the aircraft carrier Saratoga (CV-3) during World War II, 103-104

Charleston, South Carolina
    Site of the decommissioning of the patrol craft PCE(R)-858 in 1946, 240-243

Charts-Navigation
    Correction of by quartermasters on board the aircraft carrier Saratoga (CV-3) during World War II, 68-69; during World War II Germany issued corrections to its navigation charts for the benefit of mariners from neutral nations, 184

Clifton, Commander Joseph C., USN (USNA, 1930)
    Colorful naval aviator who served as the commander of Carrier Air Group 12 in the aircraft carrier Saratoga (CV-3) in 1943-44, 166-169

Coast Guard, U.S.
    Movie star Victor Mature moved up rapidly as an enlisted man in the Coast Guard in World War II, 141-142

Cobb, Tyrus R.
    Hall of fame baseball player who went unrecognized during an airplane flight in 1944, 189-190

Coco Solo, Panama Canal Zone
    The patrol craft PCE(R)-858 had trouble finding her way around the harbor during a visit in 1946, 239-240

Colombo, Ceylon
Liberty opportunities for visiting American sailors in early 1944, 155-158

Commercial Ships
See Merchant Ships

Communications
The aircraft carrier Saratoga (CV-3) used cumbersome flag hoists used when operating with the British Far Eastern Fleet in the Indian Ocean in early 1944, 145-146, 149; problems with the radio in the patrol craft PCE(R)-858 in early 1946, 240-242

Compasses
Compensation of the magnetic compasses in the aircraft carrier Saratoga (CV-3) during World War II, 69-70

Cook, Lieutenant Commander Ozias B., CHC, USN
Role as the ship's chaplain in the aircraft carrier Saratoga (CV-3) during World War II, 103-104

Corsair
Norwegian-built yacht that was used for training Sea Scouts around Long Beach, California, in the early 1940s, 4-7, 9-10

Courts-Martial
Cases of homosexual activity and acceptance of bribes were tried by courts on board the aircraft carrier Saratoga (CV-3) in 1943, 97-100

Derry, Chief Gunner's Mate Harold L., USN
Was advanced to chief petty officer in World War II as a result of winning a fistfight with Captain Gerald Bogan, commanding officer of the aircraft carrier Saratoga (CV-3), 102-103

Discipline
Methods used by a no-nonsense chief petty officer at boot camp in San Diego in 1942, 31-32; courts-martial on board the aircraft carrier Saratoga (CV-3) in 1943, 97-100; two commanding officers of the Saratoga (CV-3) took different approaches when handing out punishment for drinking-related offenses in World War II, 101-102

Dutch Navy
Supplied warships for operation with the British Far Eastern Fleet in the Indian Ocean in early 1944, 147-148

Education
　　Bond's experiences in schools in California in the 1930s and 1940s, 14-15; Bond's education at the University of Southern California following World War II, 26-27, 237, 245-246

Engineering Plants
　　Repairs to the turbines of the aircraft carrier Saratoga (CV-3) in 1943, 113-114; speed capability of the Saratoga after her 1944 overhaul, 195

Eniwetok Atoll, Marshall Islands
　　Devastated condition after the U.S. bombardments in early 1944, 137-138

Enlisted Personnel
　　Recruit training at San Diego in 1942, 28-40; right-arm rating badges in World War II, 32; assignment to duties on the basis of classification tests, 41; relationship of officers and enlisted in the aircraft carrier Saratoga (CV-3) in World War II, 104-105, 107; movie star Victor Mature moved up rapidly as an enlisted man in the Coast Guard in World War II, 141-142; advancement procedures for petty officers on board the Saratoga in World War II, 180-182

Enterprise, USS (CV-6)
　　Rivalry with the crew of the aircraft carrier Saratoga (CV-3) in World War II, 77-78

Espiritu Santo, New Hebrides
　　Measurement of tides and currents during World War II by the crew of the aircraft carrier Saratoga (CV-3), 70

F6F Hellcat
　　Fighter plane that was introduced to the air group of the aircraft carrier Saratoga (CV-3) in late 1943, 119-120; too big for the Saratoga's after elevator to handle, 196

Fire
　　The aircraft carrier Saratoga (CV-3) suffered heavy fires after being hit by Japanese kamikazes near Iwo Jima in February 1945, 200-201

Fishing
　　Crewmen of the U.S. patrol craft PCE(R)-858 caught and sold fish to the Japanese following the end of World War II, 235-236

Fletcher, Vice Admiral Frank Jack, USN (USNA, 1906)
　　While embarked in the aircraft carrier Saratoga (CV-3) in August 1942, was impatient with counterflooding after the ship was torpedoed off Guadalcanal, 107-108

Food
Ice cream available in the ship's service fountain of the aircraft carrier Saratoga (CV-3) in the 1930s and 1940s, 3; in World War II the commanding officer of the San Diego destroyer base went through the chow line himself to ensure quality food for enlisted personnel, 43; the British aircraft carrier Victorious received a supply of dehydrated potatoes from the American carrier Saratoga (CV-3) in 1943, 79; inadequate food storage facilities in the Saratoga in World War II, 79-80; messing conditions on board the Saratoga, 87-89; a Tasmanian man was generous in providing fresh fruit to Saratoga crew members when the ship visited Hobart in 1944, 139-140, 145; the Saratoga rewarded smaller ships with ice cream when they returned downed pilots in World War II, 162-163; Royal Navy ships served tea in the afternoon with crewmen providing their own food, 175; in 1945 wily crew members of the patrol craft PCE(R)-858 stole food from locked storerooms, 225-227; the crew of the PCE(R)-858 enjoyed fine chow, 227-228, 234; crewmen of the U.S. patrol craft PCE(R)-858 sold fish to the Japanese following the end of World War II, 235-236

Football
Played in high schools in the Los Angeles area in the early 1940s, 18

French Navy
The battleship Richelieu operated with the British Far Eastern Fleet in the Indian Ocean in early 1944, 147; French warships had a reputation for being filthy, 184

GI Bill
Role in financing Bond's college education following World War II, 245-246

Gain, Chief Quartermaster Willard M., USN
Asiatic Fleet veteran who ran the navigation division of the aircraft carrier Saratoga (CV-3) during World War II, 73, 144-145

Germany
During World War II Germany issued corrections to its navigation charts for the benefit of mariners from neutral nations, 184

Gilbert Islands
Aircraft carriers in support of the U.S. invasion of in November 1943, 130-132

Great Britain
See Royal Navy

Guadalcanal
U.S. destroyers patrolled in the Solomon Islands in late 1942 when the Japanese were running the Tokyo Express to the area, 56-62; fighter pilots sprayed the brush at the end of a runway to counteract snipers, 58; the captain and embarked flag officer in the aircraft carrier Saratoga (CV-3) disagreed about counterflooding the ship after she was torpedoed off Guadalcanal in August 1942, 107-108

See also Tulagi

Gunnery-Naval
Emphasis on gun crew training at boot camp in San Diego in 1942, 30; use of a 5-inch loading machine for training gun crews on board the destroyer Saufley (DD-465) in 1942, 51

Guns
Use of a 5-inch loading machine for training gun crews on board the destroyer Saufley (DD-465) in 1942, 51; the aircraft carrier Saratoga (CV-3) lost some 20-mm guns while in rough weather near Tasmania in 1944, 138; the main battery guns of the French battleship Richelieu, which operated with U.S. forces in World War II, could he reloaded while elevated, 147

Habitability
Messing and berthing conditions for enlisted men in the aircraft carrier Saratoga (CV-3) during World War II, 76, 79-90

Halsey, Admiral William F., Jr., USN (USNA, 1904)
As Commander South Pacific Force, went aboard the aircraft carrier Saratoga (CV-3) in late 1943 to talk to the crew about an upcoming raid on Rabaul, 115-116

Hammocks
Used for sleeping by enlisted crewmen on board the aircraft carrier Saratoga (CV-3) in World War II, 81-82

Hart, Quartermaster First Class William H., USN
Missouri man who served in the navigation division of the aircraft carrier Saratoga (CV-3) during World War II, 73-74

Hedgehogs
Antisubmarine weapons used by the patrol craft PCE(R)-858 during shakedown training in the summer of 1945, 221

Hiroshima, Japan
Condition of the city following the atomic bomb attack in 1945, 233-235

Hobart, Tasmania
Site of a port visit by the aircraft carrier Saratoga (CV-3) in early 1944, 138-140, 145

Homosexuality
Cases of homosexual activity were tried by courts-martial on board the aircraft carrier Saratoga (CV-3) in 1943, 97-99

Honolulu, Hawaii
Predominance of servicemen on liberty in Honolulu during World War II, 54-55

Hunters Point, San Francisco
Repair period for the aircraft carrier Saratoga (CV-3) in early 1944, 133

Illustrious, HMS
British aircraft carrier that operated in the Dutch East Indies in early 1944, 126, 165-166

Indian Ocean
Operations of the British Far Eastern Fleet in early 1944, 125, 145-164

Inspections
Stenciling and inspection of uniforms at boot camp in San Diego in 1942, 31, 34-35; officers of the British Far Eastern Fleet conducted a series of personnel inspections of the crew of the aircraft carrier Saratoga (CV-3) when she was operating in the Indian Ocean in early 1944, 152-154

Iwo Jima
The U.S. aircraft carrier Saratoga (CV-3) was damaged by Japanese kamikazes during the Iwo Jima campaign of February 1945, 199-203

Japan
U.S. minesweeping operations around the Japanese home islands in late 1945-early 1946, 228-233; condition of Hiroshima following the atomic bomb attack in 1945, 233-235; crew members of the patrol craft PCE(R)-858 took photos in Japan in late 1945, 233-235; crewmen of the PCE(R)-858 sold fish to Japanese people following the end of World War II, 235-236

Japanese Navy
A magazine article published around 1939-40 credited the Japanese with having the second-best aircraft carrier pilots in the world, 21-22; sinking of the U.S. gunboat

Panay (PR-5) in 1937, 22; ran the Tokyo Express to the Solomon Islands in late 1942, 56-62; the destroyer Yayoi was sunk near Tulagi in late 1942, later salvaged, 60; made surprisingly little use of submarines against merchant shipping during World War II, 61-62; curiously, the Japanese committed their aircraft only piecemeal when planes from the U.S. aircraft carrier Saratoga (CV-3) attacked Rabaul in November 1943, 119; the aircraft carrier Saratoga (CV-3) was damaged by Japanese kamikazes during the Iwo Jima campaign of February 1945, 199-203

Java
Target of Allied carrier air strike in May 1944, 165-166

Johnson, Chief Machinist's Mate Oscar, USN
Having joined the crew of the aircraft carrier Saratoga (CV-3) upon commissioning in 1927, he was still on board during World War II, 141-144

Kamikazes
The U.S. aircraft carrier Saratoga (CV-3) was damaged by Japanese kamikazes during the Iwo Jima campaign of February 1945, 199-203

Key West, Florida
Had an interesting mix of ships and personnel right after the end of World War II, 239-240

Lake Michigan
The patrol craft PCE(R)-858 plane-guarded for carrier qualifications on the lake in 1945, 214-215

Larson, Herman
Retired merchant marine captain who donated his time to the Sea Scouts around Long Beach, California, in the early 1940s, 4-7, 9-10, 21, 53; served as captain of the bark Renée Rickmers when she ran aground in New Caledonia in 1914, 8; experience between the World Wars, 9; death in 1944, 10; enlisted service in the German Navy, 12

Leave and Liberty
Recreational opportunities were few for low-paid recruits on liberty in San Diego in 1942, 44-45; Bond spent time with his future wife, Marilyn Williams, while on liberty from boot camp, 45-46; sailors from the destroyer Saufley (DD-465) rode a narrow-gauge train when on liberty in Hawaii in 1942, 53-54; predominance of servicemen on liberty in Honolulu during World War II, 54-55; crew members of the aircraft carrier Saratoga (CV-3) went ashore in Noumea, New Caledonia, in World War II, 76-77; Saratoga crew members enjoyed leave and ship's parties

while in San Francisco in early 1944, 133-136; Saratoga crew members had a pleasant port visit to Hobart, Tasmania, in early 1944, 138-140, 145; the British were generous with their beer allotment when operating a fleet out of Ceylon in early 1944, 150-151; in Colombo, Ceylon, in early 1944, 155-158; attractions in Australia during World War II, 177-179; Bond took a long leave trip home to Milwaukee when his ship was at Bremerton in the summer of 1944, 187-191; liberty in Bremerton, Washington, in 1944, 191-193; in Miami, Florida, in 1945, 210-211; U.S. servicemen went ashore in Japan following the surrender in 1945, 233-236; crewmen of the patrol craft PCE(R)-858 got to know a number of WAVES at Key West, Florida, in early 1946, 239-240

London, HMS
British cruiser that rescued an officer lost overboard from the aircraft carrier Saratoga (CV-3) in early 1944, 163

Mail
Incoming and outgoing letters for crew members of the aircraft carrier Saratoga (CV-3) during World War II, 93-94, 110-112, 150; censorship of mail, 94, 150

Mainland, Lieutenant David G., USNR
Served as executive officer and navigator of the patrol craft PCE(R)-858 for a time shortly after the end of World War II, 236-237, 242; postwar civilian career, 242-243

Maintenance
Of four-stack destroyers and S-class submarines at the San Diego destroyer base during World War II, 41-42

Marathon, USS (APA-200)
Damaged attack transport that was used in U.S. minesweeping operations around the Japanese home islands in late 1945-early 1946, 228-233

Marine Corps, U.S.
Enlisted Marines served as time orderlies and buglers in the aircraft carrier Saratoga (CV-3) during World War II, 92-93; Marines ttied to teach sailors to march on board the Saratoga in 1944, 179

Marshall Islands
Aircraft carriers in support of the U.S. invasion of in February 1944, 137-138; devastated condition after Eniwetok the U.S. bombardments in early 1944, 137-138

Matecki, Seaman First Class Leo C., USN
Chicago sailor who served in the aircraft carrier Saratoga (CV-3) in World War II, later returned to his hometown, 214

Mature, Chief Boatswain's Mate Victor, USCGR
Movie star who moved up rapidly in the Coast Guard of World War II, 141-142

McCandless, Captain Byron, USN (Ret.) (USNA, 1905)
Energetic and unpredictable as the commanding officer of the San Diego destroyer base during World War II, 42-43

Medical Problems
Bond contracted a case of pneumonia while in the South Pacific in the spring of 1943, 62-64

Merchant Ships
In the early years of the century merchant sailing ships of various nations had similar rigging because of the international nature of their crews, 7-8

See also Corsair, Renée Rickmers

Michigan, Lake
See Lake Michigan

Miami, Florida
Site of Navy subchaser training during World War II, 209-211; liberty opportunities for sailors in 1945, 210-211

Milwaukee, Wisconsin
Hospitable city for visiting servicemen in World War II, 187-189

Minesweeping
U.S. minesweeping operations around the Japanese home islands in late 1945-early 1946, 228-233

Mississippi River
The patrol craft PCE(R)-858 made a transit from Chicago to New Orleans in the spring of 1945, 216-220

Moebus, Captain Lucian A., USN (USNA, 1921)
Commanded the aircraft carrier Saratoga (CV-3) in 1944-45, 123-124, 201-202

Mountbatten, Admiral Lord Louis, RN
Made an inspiring speech to the crew when he visited the aircraft carrier Saratoga (CV-3) in early 1944, 153-155

Movies
    Shown on board the British battleship <u>Valiant</u> during World War II, 174-176; shown on board the aircraft carrier <u>Saratoga</u> (CV-3) in World War II, 187

Mullinnix, Rear Admiral Henry M., USN (USNA, 1916)
    As commanding officer of the aircraft carrier <u>Saratoga</u> (CV-3) in 1943, was lenient on men who committed drinking-related offenses, 101-102; died in November 1943, 102, 130-131

Naval Academy, U.S., Annapolis, Maryland
    A midshipman named John Rough resigned from the academy prior to graduation with the class of 1916, later gave his class ring to Bond for World War II, 13-14

Naval Reserve, U.S.
    The organization of the reserve in the years after World War II discouraged Bond from taking part, 251

Navigation
    Work of the small navigation division in the aircraft carrier <u>Saratoga</u> (CV-3) during World War II, 67-75, 90-92, 100, 182-185; correction of navigation charts, 68-69, 182-184; compensation of the magnetic compasses in the <u>Saratoga</u>, 69-70; celestial navigation in the <u>Saratoga</u>, 71; problems with radar navigation when the patrol craft <u>PCE(R)-858</u> arrived at Charleston, South Carolina, in early 1946, 241-242

New Caledonia
    The merchant sailing ship <u>Renée Rickmers</u> ran aground in New Caledonia in 1914 because the French had blacked out the lighthouse there, 8; part of the wreck was still visible in World War II, 8-9; crew members of the aircraft carrier <u>Saratoga</u> (CV-3) went on liberty in Noumea in World War II, 76-77

New Orleans, Louisiana
    Site of shipyard work for the patrol craft <u>PCE(R)-858</u> in the summer of 1945, 220-221

Nuclear Weapons
    Condition of Hiroshima, Japan, following the atomic bomb attack in 1945, 233-235

Okinawa
    Operations around this island by the patrol craft <u>PCE(R)-858</u> in 1945, 228, 232

PCE(R)-858, USS
    Patrol craft manned by inexperienced junior officers when she went into commission in 1945, 1-7, 129, 212-213;

ship's characteristics, 211-212, 221; transit from Chicago to New Orleans in the spring of 1945, 216-220; shipyard work in New Orleans, 220-221; shakedown in the summer of 1945, 221-222; the ship was repainted frequently in 1945-46, 222-223; Panama Canal transits in 1945-46, 223-225, 238; brief stop at Pearl Harbor, 225; thefts of food by wily crew members, 225-227; the crew enjoyed fine chow, 227-228, 234; operations around Okinawa in 1945, 228, 232; support of minesweeping operations around Japan in 1945, 228-231; crew members took photos in Japan in late 1945, 233-235; crewmen caught and sold fish to the Japanese following the end of World War II, 235-236; ship's return to the United States, 237-240; went to Charleston, South Carolina, for decommissioning in 1946, 240-243

Panama Canal
Damaged when the aircraft carrier Saratoga (CV-3) made her first transit through the canal in the late 1920s, 142-143; canal transit by the patrol craft PCE(R)-858 in 1945, 223-225

Pay and Allowances
In 1942 the initial pay for Navy recruits was low, particularly after deductions, 44

Pearl Harbor, Hawaii
Damage wrought by the Japanese attack in December 1941 was still evident more than a year later, 48-49; liberty for the crew of the destroyer Saufley (DD-465) in 1942, 53-54; details of conning the ship when the aircraft carrier Saratoga (CV-3) arrived at Pearl during World War II, 127-128; brief visit by the PCE(R)-858 in 1945, 129, 225

Photography
Crew members of the U.S. patrol craft PCE(R)-858 took photos in Japan in late 1945, 233-235

Princeton, USS (CVL-23)
Light carrier that supported amphibious operations in the northern Solomons in late 1943, 115; problems with steering gear during Gilbert Islands invasion in November 1943, 132

Puget Sound Navy Yard, Bremerton, Washington
The Craven Center provided varied forms of recreation for Navy personnel during World War II, 47, 192-193; overhauled the aircraft carrier Saratoga (CV-3) in the summer of 1944, 122, 190-194

Rabaul, New Britain
Site of a Japanese base that was attacked by planes from the aircraft carrier Saratoga (CV-3) in November 1943, 115-120, 164-165

Radar
Because of her large sail area, the aircraft carrier Saratoga (CV-3) was particularly susceptible to radar detection in World War II, 152; during a kamikaze attack in February 1945, the radar of the Saratoga mistakenly identified Japanese planes as friendly, 201-203; problems with radar navigation when the patrol craft PCE(R)-858 arrived at Charleston, South Carolina, in early 1946, 241-242

Railroads
Sailors from the destroyer Saufley (DD-465) rode a narrow-gauge train when on liberty in Hawaii in 1942, 53-54; Bond was part of a draft of sailors that took chartered railroad cars from California to Florida in 1945, 207-209; cross-country train trip to California when Bond was discharged in 1946, 243-244

Ramsey, Captain Dewitt C., USN (USNA, 1912)
As commanding officer of the aircraft carrier Saratoga (CV-3) during the invasion of Guadalcanal in August 1942, tangled with the embarked flag officer, Vice Admiral Frank Jack Fletcher, 107-108

Recruiting
A chief petty officer in Beverly Hills, California, recruited Bond and a friend into the Navy in 1942, 25-26

Recruit Training
Orientation and testing at boot camp at San Diego in 1942, 28; emphasis on gunnery training, 30; stenciling and inspection of uniforms, 31, 34-35; living conditions in barracks, 33-34; recruits had varied backgrounds, 35; swimming tests, 35-36; rifle range practice, 36-37; curriculum, 38-40; classification tests, 41; recreational opportunities were few for low-paid recruits on liberty in San Diego in 1942, 44-48

Refueling
When the aircraft carrier Saratoga (CV-3) operated with the British Far Eastern Fleet in 1944, she was faster than the Royal Navy ships in refueling at sea, 126

Religion
Role of Lieutenant Commander Ozias B. Cook as ship's chaplain in the aircraft carrier Saratoga (CV-3) during World War II, 103-104

Relocation Camps
   Japanese-Americans were sent to internment camps soon after the United States entered World War II in 1941, 18-19

Renée Rickmers
   Merchant sailing ship that piled up on the barrier reef at New Caledonia in 1914; part of the wreck was still visible in World War II, 8-9

Rescue at Sea
   The British submarine Tactician rescued a fighter pilot downed in a raid on Sabang in early 1944, 162; the British cruiser London picked up a man who fell overboard from the aircraft carrier Saratoga (CV-3) in 1944, 163

Richelieu
   French battleship that operated with the British Far Eastern Fleet in the Indian Ocean in early 1944, 147

Rough, Midshipman John, USN
   Even though he was part of the class of 1916 at the Naval Academy, he dropped out prior to graduation and later gave his class ring to Bond in World War II, 13-14

Royal Navy
   The carrier Victorious operated with the U.S. Navy during the New Georgia campaign of 1943, 79; the Victorious received a supply of dehydrated potatoes from the American carrier Saratoga (CV-3), 79; operations of the British Far Eastern Fleet in the Indian Ocean in early 1944, 125, 145-164; tropical white uniforms worn by Royal Navy personnel when the British were operating in the Indian Ocean, 152-153; Admiral Lord Louis Mountbatten made an inspiring speech to the crew when he visited the Saratoga (CV-3) in early 1944, 153-155; operations in the Dutch East Indies, 165-166, 171-173; Royal Navy ships served tea in the afternoon with crewmen providing their own food, 175

SBD Dauntless
   Dive bomber used by the aircraft carrier Saratoga (CV-3) in late 1943, 116-118

Sabang
   Site of Allied carrier strike in April 1944, 161-162

Salvage
   The Japanese destroyer Yayoi was sunk at Tulagi in late 1942, later salvaged by the U.S. Navy, 60

San Diego, California
Site of Navy recruit training in 1942, 28-40; maintenance of four-stack destroyers and S-class submarines at the destroyer base during World War II, 41-42; recreational opportunities were few for low-paid recruits on liberty in San Diego in 1942, 44-48

San Francisco, California
Crew members of the aircraft carrier Saratoga (CV-3) enjoyed leave and ship's parties while in the city in early 1944, 133-134

Saratoga, USS (CV-3)
Aircraft carrier visited by civilians in the 1930s, 2-3; the navigator gave Bond a job interview for quartermaster in 1943, 15; big job involved in painting the flight deck, 64-65; work of the navigation division, 67-75, 90-92, 100, 182-185; compensation of the magnetic compasses, 69-70; messing and berthing conditions for the enlisted crew members, 76, 79-90; forms of recreation for the crew in World War II, 76-77; rivalry with the crew of the carrier Enterprise (CV-6), 77-78; operation in the New Georgia campaign in 1943, 79; only carrier with a conning tower, 90-91; incoming and outgoing mail, 93-94, 110-112, 150; time in the ship's brig was unpleasant, 94-95; operations out of the New Hebrides in the summer of 1943, 95-96, air group, 96; cases of homosexual activity and acceptance of bribes were tried by courts-martial on board the ship in 1943, 97-100; Captain Gerald F. Bogan as skipper in 1942-43, 101-102; Captain Henry M. Mullinnix as skipper in 1943, 101-102; role of the ship's chaplain, 103-104; relationship of officers and enlisted, 104-105, 107; anchoring and mooring procedures, 105-107; torpedoed off Guadalcanal in August 1942, 107-108; speed of, 112-115, 163-164, 195; operations in the Solomons in late 1943, 113-115; Captain John H. Cassady as skipper in 1943-44, 113-114, 121-125, 127-130, 133, 138, 151-152, 163-164, 201; the air group conducted raids on Rabaul, New Britain, in November 1943, 115-120, 164-165; underwent overhaul at the Puget Sound Navy Yard in the summer of 1944, 122, 190-194; Captain Lucian A. Moebus as skipper in 1944-45, 123-124, 201-202; operations with the British Far Eastern Fleet in early 1944, 125, 145-166, 171-173; the ship's handling qualities, 126-127; support of the invasion of the Gilbert Islands in late 1943, 130-132; ship's parties and leave during repair period in San Francisco in early 1944, 133-136; transported a group of Seabees from California to Hawaii in 1944, 136-137; support of Marshall Islands invasion in February 1944, 137-138; lost 20-mm guns in heavy seas, 138; visit to Tasmania, 138-140, 145; some of the original 1927 crewmen were still on board in World War II, 141-144; damaged the

Panama Canal in the late 1920s, 142-143; Admiral Lord Louis Mountbatten made an inspiring speech to the crew when he visited the ship in early 1944, 153-155; cleaning and wearing of uniforms on board, 159-161; race against British ships, 163-164; Commander Joseph Clifton was a colorful naval aviator who commanded the ship's air group in 1943-44, 166-169; drinking on board ship in World War II, 169-171; advancement procedures for enlisted men, 180-182; steering procedures, 185-187; operated around Hawaii in late 1944-early 1945, 196; operations around Japan and Iwo Jima in early 1945, 197-198; damaged by Japanese kamikazes during the Iwo Jima campaign of February 1945, 199-203; burial at sea for those killed by kamikazes, 203-204; former crew members had their own American Legion post after World War II, 251-252; before World War II two of the ship's chief petty officers kept a boat in the Puget Sound area for recreation, 254

Saufley, USS (DD-465)
Destroyer that had a top speed close to 40 knots during World War II, 50; use of a 5-inch loading machine for training gun crews in 1942, 51; shellback initiation in 1942, 53; liberty in Hawaii for the crew, 53-54; operations around the Solomons in late 1942, 56-62; made one unsuccessful antisubmarine attack, 62, large engineering plant, 86

Seabees
A group of construction battalion members experienced a great deal of seasickness while riding the aircraft carrier Saratoga (CV-3) from California to Hawaii in 1944, 136-137

Seadrift
Yacht that operated out of southern California, taken into Coast Guard service for World War II, 15-16

Sea Scouts
A retired merchant marine captain named Herman Larson donated his time to the Sea Scouts around Long Beach, California, in the early 1940s, 4-7, 9-10, 21, 53

Seasickness
A group of construction battalion members experienced a great deal of seasickness while riding the aircraft carrier Saratoga (CV-3) from California to Hawaii in 1944, 136-137

Sherman, Rear Admiral Frederick C., USN (USNA, 1910)
Embarked in the aircraft carrier Saratoga (CV-3) in 1943 while serving as a carrier division commander, 109, 115, 119, 130-132, 197

Shiphandling
Conning of the aircraft carrier Saratoga (CV-3) by Captain John Cassady in 1943-44, 113-114, 124-125, 127-129, 151-152, 163-164; handling qualities of the Saratoga in World War II, 126-127; handling of the PCE(R)-858 by an inexperienced captain when she arrived at Pearl Harbor in 1945, 129

Shryer, Quartermaster Second Class Leslie, USN
Intelligent individual who served in the navigation division of the aircraft carrier Saratoga (CV-3) during World War II, 74; on liberty in Hobart, Tasmania, in early 1944, 139-140

Solomon Islands
U.S. destroyers patrolled in the region in late 1942 when the Japanese were running the Tokyo Express to the area, 56-62; the Japanese destroyer Yayoi was sunk at Tulagi in late 1942, later salvaged by the U.S. Navy, 60; the aircraft carriers Saratoga (CV-3) and Princeton (CVL-23) supported amphibious operations in the northern Solomons in late 1943, 113-115

Southern California, University of, Los Angeles
Site of Bond's college education following his discharge from the Navy in 1946, 26-27, 237, 245-246

Swimming
Many of the recruits had trouble with swimming while undergoing boot camp training at San Diego in 1942, 35-36

Tactician, HMS
British submarine that rescued a downed fighter pilot at Sabang in April 1944, 161-162

Tactics
Curiously, the Japanese committed their aircraft only piecemeal when planes from the U.S. aircraft carrier Saratoga (CV-3) attacked Rabaul in November 1943, 119

Tasmania
Hobart was the site of a port visit by the aircraft carrier Saratoga (CV-3) in early 1944, 138-140, 145

Training
A retired merchant marine captain named Herman Larson gave seamanship training to Sea Scouts around Long Beach, California, in the early 1940s, 4-7, 9-10, 21, 53; recruit training at San Diego in 1942, 28-40; use of a 5-inch loading machine for training gun crews on board the destroyer Saufley (DD-465) in 1942, 51; on-the-job

quartermaster school on board the aircraft carrier Saratoga (CV-3) in World War II, 72; shakedown cruise for the patrol craft PCE(R)-858 in the summer of 1945, 221-222

Trincomalee, Ceylon
Served as a base for the aircraft carrier Saratoga (CV-3) when she was operating with the British Far Eastern Fleet in early 1944, 125, 146, 150-151, 157, 173-174

Tulagi, Solomon Islands
The Japanese destroyer Yayoi was sunk at Tulagi in late 1942, later salvaged by the U.S. Navy, 60

Uniforms-Naval
A few U.S. Navy enlisted men still had dress-white uniforms during World War II, 23; stenciling and inspection of uniforms at boot camp in San Diego in 1942, 31; tropical white uniforms worn by Royal Navy personnel when the British Far Eastern Fleet was operating in the Indian Ocean in early 1944, 152-153; cleaning and wearing of uniforms on board the aircraft carrier Saratoga (CV-3) during World War II, 159-161

Valiant, HMS
British battleship that operated in the Indian Ocean in early 1944, 150-151; a member of the ship's crew had a considerable capacity for beer, 173-174; living conditions on board for the crew, 174-176

Victorious, HMS
British aircraft carrier that operated with the U.S. Navy during the New Georgia campaign of 1943, 79; received a supply of dehydrated potatoes from the American carrier Saratoga (CV-3), 79

Visual Signaling
The aircraft carrier Saratoga (CV-3) used cumbersome flag hoists used when operating with the British Far Eastern Fleet in the Indian Ocean in early 1944, 145-146, 149

WAVES
Crewmen of the patrol craft PCE(R)-858 got to know a number of Navy women in social situations at Key West, Florida, in early 1946, 239-240

Weather
A group of construction battalion members experienced a great deal of seasickness while riding the aircraft carrier Saratoga (CV-3) through heavy seas while en route from California to Hawaii in 1944, 136-137; the Saratoga ran into heavy seas while en route Tasmania in early 1944, 138

Wolverine, USS (IX-64)
    Converted passenger ship used for qualification of carrier pilots on Lake Michigan in World War II, 214-215

Yayoi (Japanese Destroyer)
    Sunk at Tulagi in the Solomon Islands in late 1942, later salvaged by the U.S. Navy, 60

www.ingramcontent.com/pod-product-compliance
Lightning Source LLC
Chambersburg PA
CBHW080616170426
43209CB00007B/1444